BILL JOHNSON

CENTER

OF THE

UNIVERSE

*A Look at Life
from the Lighter Side*

DESTINY IMAGE® PUBLISHERS, INC.

P.O. Box 310, Shippensburg, PA 17257-0310

"Speaking to the Purposes of God for This Generation and for the Generations to Come."

This book and all other Destiny Image, Revival Press, MercyPlace, Fresh Bread, Destiny Image Fiction, and Treasure House books are available at Christian bookstores and distributors worldwide.

For a U.S. bookstore nearest you, call 1-800-722-6774.

For more information on foreign distributors, call 717-532-3040.

Reach us on the Internet: www.destinyimage.com.

Trade Paper ISBN: 978-0-7684-3610-5

Hardcover ISBN: 978-0-7684-3611-2

Large Print ISBN: 978-0-7684-3612-9

Ebook ISBN: 978-0-7684-9050-3

For Worldwide Distribution, Printed in the U.S.A.

2 3 4 5 6 7 8 / 14 13 12 11

DEDICATION

I dedicate this book to the spiritual leaders at Mountain Chapel in Weaverville, California. The impact of their lives will only be seen in eternity. Thanks, with much love!

ACKNOWLEDGMENTS

Much thanks goes to Allison Amerding, Pam Spinosi, and Mary Walker for helping me with the edit. Special thanks to Don Milam for his willingness and desire to put this into print.

Contents

INTRODUCTION

Center of the Universe might seem like a strange title for a book. Especially considering the inspiration for the title was a town of 3,500 people. But faith looks at things a bit differently than reason, as faith lives from the unseen.

I began to pastor in the community of Weaverville, California, in 1978. Like most young men, I was filled with vision and hope for what God could do, even in a small community. My challenge to the people was rather simple—let's change the world.

I couldn't stand the idea of moving to a city "where the elephants go to die." The mentality in such places doesn't lend itself to shaping the course of world history. When I became the pastor, I immediately started teaching on the significance of anyone who will believe God. If I could shift the attitude of the church, anything was possible.

The challenge was clear—if you live in a city of millions, the devil will tell you that you are only one person, and therefore insignificant. If you're in a small community, the devil says the whole place is insignificant. But one person and God is a majority, which means there is no such thing as an insignificant person or city. Not even the devil seemed concerned about anything good coming from Weaverville. That meant our efforts would ambush his by honoring our King through faith-filled endeavors. I began to refer to Weaverville as "The Center of the Universe." It was my humorous way of expressing a true, burning conviction.

It's important for you to believe the same for your city and your life. Only then will we take the risks necessary to help impact the nations of the world for Christ.

My daughter-in-law, Candace, suggested the title for this book. She had heard the stories of how I often referred to Weaverville, California, as the center of the universe. It just seemed appropriate, as it bears my conviction, with a bit of tongue and cheek thrown in for good measure. It really does represent how I view wherever we live and the potential impact of our partnership with God.

Many told me to put these articles into a book, but I always downplayed such words. My own mother was the strongest voice in this regard. My secretary always mailed the bulletin to my parents every week. Mom kept them all, of course.

Almost on a whim one day I sent the entire PDF file of articles to my friend and agent Don Milam with Destiny Image Publishers. He loved them and asked permission to put them into print. I was happily surprised and agreed.

Center of the Universe is a collection of humorous stories and lessons on life. Relax and enjoy.

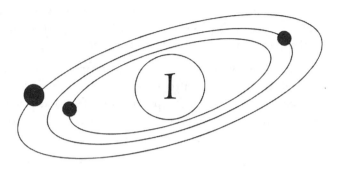

THE INSIDE

I had an unusual desire to write as a young man. But my education didn't lend itself to such a desire. In fact I was almost embarrassed to have a dream of that nature. I didn't qualify, and I knew it.

It was never my intention to dishonor God, nor did I want to waste His time. If He didn't want me to write, He needed to tell me. So I prayed and prayed and prayed about this dream. At this stage in my life I didn't know that God was the one who put that dream into my heart. Plus, the fear of failure had a great effect on my biggest dreams. But I knew enough to pray. And things slowly changed.

In the final season of prayer over this issue, God spoke to me clearly. This became my moment of breakthrough. In the middle of the night, His voice woke me saying, "Isaiah thirty, verse eight." I woke up and thought, *Wow, that was clear.* I opened my Bible to Isaiah 30:8, which says, *"Now, go, write...."* He said, "Yes!"

It's exciting to get permission to pursue a dream. Yet I was always better at dreaming than pursuing, especially about something for which I was so ill equipped. It was obvious to me that I couldn't sit down and write the next great American novel. I also knew that articles for major Christian magazines were out of the question. "Bill who?" And I didn't feel I had enough insight for a book. So I got the idea for *The Inside*, which was a place on the *inside* of our weekly church bulletin that was perfect for a small article. This became my communication to our church family. It would give me the chance to share my heart as well as grow in the discipline of writing. And so a great journey began.

The impact on the church was surprising and immediate. The encouraging words about *The Inside* articles came to me week after week, even from accomplished authors who had become part of our fellowship. It's hard to imagine getting too much encouragement, so I kept all these words dear to my heart. News got around and we had people who attended other churches asking for copies of our bulletin. Even spouses who didn't attend church would ask their family members to bring a copy home.

My focus was always to communicate truth. But this particular avenue seemed to lend itself to fun. And so I wrote week after week about some unusual or embarrassing experience, a funny story, or some trivial glimpse into my life. It was therapeutic for me, and uplifting for the church. And it launched me on the quest to learn to write—one I am still on.

This journey with *The Inside* started in the late 1980s and ended with my departure from Weaverville in February 1996.

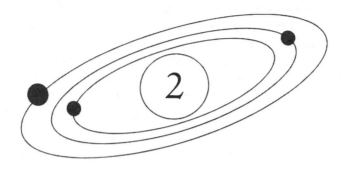

A Time for Things to Break

We had been looking forward to attending my dog's field trials for quite some time. About one month ago, we finally had the opportunity. On the way, our windshield wipers quit working—in the middle of a Sacramento Valley downpour. We drove for about 35 miles, mostly on the side of the road, peeking through the 2-inch semi-clear opening immediately above the wiper. Such an experience can give you a whole new release in your prayer language. A mechanic at Yuba City gas station was able to get them going again, and they lasted until we got home.

Two weeks ago our dryer decided to give up the ghost. Our washer, while technically still alive, had made an appointment with Dr. Kevorkian. Although Beni and I had decided not to buy Christmas gifts for each other this year, our plans changed. We decided to buy what we've always wanted: two Super Capacity Whirlpools.

Eric's truck wasn't running properly and needed some minor repairs. After more than $300 it runs great, although it wouldn't start this morning. It looks like it's the battery this time.

Brian received a stereo cassette deck for his car for Christmas. His speakers were defective. Speaker set number two was defective. He changed brands and tried what was considered to be one of the finest pairs you can buy. Surprise, surprise, they were also defective. We went to our third store and tried set number four yesterday. As he opened the box, we discovered what ended up being a defect in one of the finest speakers that he could have hoped to own. Is he doing something wrong? No. Speakers are easy to hook up. These are actual defects that I've seen with my own eyes and heard with my own ears.

We received a microwave oven from my wife's parents this Christmas. It was one of the finer brands. Our small unit had died about a year ago. It was going to be nice to have one in the house again, especially this large capacity unit. It worked for one night. The next morning it was as though it wasn't even plugged in. Nothing worked, not even the clock. My father-in-law took it back and picked out another one. We excitedly brought the new one home. It worked for one night as well. Yesterday we exchanged it for our third microwave this week. As of this morning we have a microwave oven that has worked for a whole night without incident. Of course, we're a little nervous about using it. But at least we have one, and the clock works. Should we get brave enough to actually use it for cooking, we'll find out if it will last.

Since writing the above sentence, we used the microwave. It worked once, and is now dead.

Opening gifts is always fun, especially for parents. This last spring we purchased a video camera to capture the memories of those wonderful moments on film. This is the first Christmas we have had our little Panasonic. My young nephew also liked my camera. And when he dropped it, he allowed us to see if the warranty will cover the results of the law of gravity. Yesterday it was mailed to the repair store in Illinois, with our jammed tape included. They say we'll get the tape back.

Last night I tried to console my son about his speakers. He had spent four days installing a stereo that should have taken a couple of hours. I reminded him of the need to give thanks in all situations, as well as to learn the important lesson of how unimportant possessions are. As I gave him my words of encouragement, I was holding a freshly brewed cup of French Roast coffee, which I dropped. No problem, you can always brew another cup…except that it was in my favorite porcelain cup, of which I have only one. It broke and is now in the trash. I would rather not have the opportunity to live my sermons with such fresh, on-the-spot examples.

Solomon once wrote an interesting list of things like, *"…A time to love, and a time to hate; a time of war and a time of peace"* (Eccles. 3:1-8). Had he been with me this month, he would have written about a time for things to break. During such seasons I look to see if there are reasons for this weirdness. Is there sin? Is this the devourer? We tithe and give offerings. I suppose I could guess a number of causes. But when I do that, it feels more like I'm on a witch-hunt. As I've prayed about this, I come up with nothing—except how much God loves me. He loves me so much that He helps me to remember that possessions never make up a life. Only the things that affect eternity should receive my affection.

I'm thankful for the material things that help to make my life comfortable and fun. But fresh in my mind is the understanding that material things are only temporal. Even in a time when things don't seem to go well, Jesus is Lord. And for this I give thanks. Actually, while these situations and more are true, we had a wonderful Christmas. Plus, today I'm going to get a new microwave!

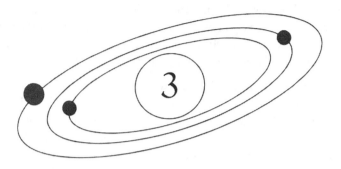

DIVINE DISTRACTIONS

His eyes were flames of fire. Out of his mouth came a sword. He just had the wrong fire, and the wrong sword—a very troubled individual indeed.

This not-so-gentle man had quite a few *visitors* on board. He reminded me somewhat of the man of the Gadarenes. The person in that biblical story fell at the feet of Jesus wanting help. The man in my story wanted to *help me*. And so, he rebuked me in the middle of my teaching. He also declared, "Ichabod!" over me and the meeting. Ichabod means, "The glory has departed." His glory had certainly departed long ago.

This gathering of 300 to 400 people was enraged that such a thing would happen. Many of them rose in my defense. One of the churches with a lot of new converts was especially upset. Most of them are right off the streets from a life of drugs and crime. They are a fresh bunch—my favorite kind. Many of them stood to their feet shouting their rebukes in return. Their zeal was strong. If they had had swords, they probably would have cut off one of his ears—possibly right to the left of his nose.

There are two kinds of conflict that I thrive on. I don't mean that I actually like them, or that I would in any way pursue them, but I must admit they have a certain element that I enjoy. The first is the battle between light and darkness. When you enter a room and turn on a light, darkness leaves. It's automatic. It's a law. When I'm under the anointing of God, very little is fearful. He promised to give us the words we need, at our moment of need. I can testify that He is faithful to His promise.

The second struggle that can be good is dealing with fighting Christians who honestly want to do God's will. With a heart that is genuinely seeking after God, they respond well to truth. And it's always fun to feed the hungry. My conflict with "Mr. Ichabod" had both elements: light vs. darkness and hungry Christians.

While no preacher wants to be interrupted, God sometimes brings certain problems out into the open during a meeting where the anointing is great and the power of unity is in effect. And when God is not the one who brings the stuff into the open, He is big enough to overpower the attempt of darkness to derail the service.

I am chief among those who do not like interruptions. But Jesus had all kinds of disturbances when He ministered. People who were sick would shout His name to get His attention, friends of the sick would tear open the roof of the home where He was meeting, the demonized would cry out and make a scene, and even the religious folks would get into the act and bring sinners before Him for judgment. His life seemed to be one big meeting with constant distractions. One well-known author calls them "divine appointments."

We like our meetings to be comfortable. We enjoy knowing what's going to happen next. This renewal has reintroduced us to a life of godly distractions. All around the world people have become uncomfortable, and some have looked for other churches to attend. Some have even invented reasonable doctrine to justify their departure from biblical standards. After all, it can be scary to have demonic manifestations while we are supposed to be worshiping God or learning from His Word. But maybe we should really be concerned if *nothing* happens when we gather in His name. His life and ministry remain the standard by which we measure all things. And He doesn't seem too upset by such interruptions.

The Holy Spirit is restoring us to a Spirit-controlled meeting, and a Spirit-controlled life! Remember, He is the Comforter. Many of us have become comforted by our own ability to control a situation or even by our knowledge of *how things ought to be*. In this hour we are being forced to receive our comfort from the Comforter.

Do you remember how many times God says, *"Do not fear"* in the Scriptures? Frequently that command came after God appeared or worked in some unexpected way. The people were given the command not to fear because fear was the most natural response to have in that setting. Not fearing was a supernatural response, the result of being open to the work of the Holy Spirit Himself. God uses divine distractions to expose the resistance that many of us have to receive our help continually from Him.

God is taking us back to His way of doing things. It's uncomfortable for those who try to assimilate everything through their own logic and reasoning. On the other hand, it's refreshing and encouraging for all who embrace this journey through the ongoing personal ministry of the Holy Spirit.

"Mr. Ichabod" left the meeting, shaking the dust off his feet. Thankfully, he took all his critters with him. His outburst came right after I read from Isaiah 35, about the unclean not being able to walk on the Highway of Holiness in a day of renewal. Little did I know that God had planned to illustrate His Word to His church. My only job was to settle the people and direct them into a redemptive act—praying for the mercy of God to visit that man.

Since it's not possible to prepare adequately for all the surprises that God may have for us, we must turn our attention to the Holy Spirit Himself. He always knows what's coming.

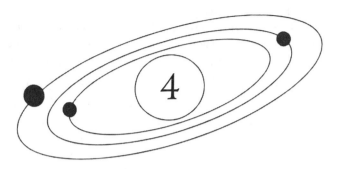

Embrace Change

Several years ago my wife and I had dinner with friends who lived on a ranch. They had a couple of horses, one of which liked to run a lot. In fact, they had to keep it in a small corral, or it would run itself to death. It's hard to comprehend that kind of love for running.

What I know about horses and how to ride them would fit into one small paragraph. In spite of my ignorance (or maybe because of it), they asked me if I'd like to ride the *runner*. I don't know if it was ego, a sense of adventure, or simple stupidity, but I accepted their invitation.

This horse ran like it was on fire. It's funny what crosses your mind when you're riding on a horse at the speed of sound through a field. I questioned my sanity and my intelligence. But uppermost on my mind was survival.

The large pasture I rode across had many holes and ruts. Because of this, the horse would frequently lose its footing, just slightly. But when you're going that fast, such things are amplified—and I was concerned. I've seen the sports bloopers where the jockey would fall and the horse would fall on top of him. No thanks. Horses are big. Besides, falling at that speed would make me similar to a rock skipping across a pond, if by some chance he missed landing on me.

Horses are supposed to be dumb. I was dumber. And the horse was well aware of that fact. After running faster than I thought possible, it turned and headed back toward my wife and friends (none of whom, I might add, had the look of concern that I thought they should have). On the way, I spotted a tree with low-hanging limbs. I tried to turn the horse's head from that direction, but it wasn't about to take directions from a rookie. I quickly learned how to melt into horsehide, lie prostrate, and pray, all the while staying attached to a saddle. The branches scraped across my back, but I was unhurt. Seeing that I survived the tree, the horse was willing to take my lead and go back to the owners. I climbed off the horse and said, "Wow! That was great!" I didn't lie. Remember, "great" was the word used to describe the San Francisco earthquake in the early 1900s.

God gave me a word at the beginning of this year—"Embrace change." Change is a lot like the mentioned horse ride: wild, fast, with holes, ruts, and obstacles, some with low-hanging branches. But it's the only way to get to where you want to be. Somebody said, "If you always do things the way you've always done them, you'll always be where you are now." And so, change is often in order.

Israel would have never considered going to a *promised land* if they weren't first dissatisfied with their immediate surroundings and circumstances. God prepared them for change by increasing pressure in their slavery. He also brought in the positive aspect of change by promising them a new land. He gave them hope. Either pressure or hope can work to ready us for change. Pressure and hope together work almost to guarantee our agreement with God on the issue.

It's interesting as a pastor to watch people come and go. Many are added to our numbers because they come and hear a word of hope. We speak often of the promises of God, which makes people aware of *divine possibilities.* In turn, they anticipate God doing a wondrous work in their lives, so they embrace the difficult challenge of change. But when the initial edge of dissatisfaction is gone, the drive for change goes with it. Why? Change is hard. It's uncomfortable. It creates a sense of deep insecurity in many people. (Remember, many a woman continues to live in an abusive situation because *at least they know what to expect.* For them, making a change creates insecurity because of the unknown.) The ones who stop *adding faith to the word they hear* (see Heb. 4:2) often become embittered toward the ones who continually speak of hope—sometimes seeking fellowship elsewhere.

I've never lived in a time when I was more aware of God requiring change in the church than now. While I'm uncomfortable with change, I'm much too dissatisfied with the status quo to stand in opposition. Plus, I'm not yet what I want to be. I've not accomplished what is in my heart to accomplish, so I welcome God's mandate for change. When He's in charge, it's always for the better. And I'm into *better!*

There's a difference between *Christianity* and *Christendom. Christianity* is the true gospel. *Christendom* is the culture developed by Christians—sometimes filled with traditions and practices that have nothing to do with the real thing. The mandate for change is God desiring us to move from the Christian *culture* we've created and return to a true *gospel.* Yes, it's a wild ride. But once you've embraced His promises, nothing else will do.

As Steven Curtis Chapman sings, "Saddle up your horses." You might also want to buckle your seatbelts.

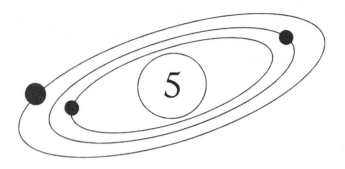

Preparing for Revival

Believers from almost every denomination are praying for revival. While the definitions from each group may vary, our common ground is that revival is a *visitation of God*. The Book of Acts illustrates that visitation should be evidenced by three witnesses. **Character**—the righteousness of Jesus seen through us in practical Christian living; **Power**—a demonstration of God for personal victory over ailments of life, both spiritual and natural; and **Converts**—unbelievers committing their lives to Christ. Since all revivals are ultimately initiated by God stirring the church to pray, we can assume that a great time of visitation is in His plans for this hour.

Understanding the cycle of revivals throughout history can help us to ready ourselves for what could become the greatest revival of all time. The spiritual showers we see today are preparatory for the great outpouring that should soon follow. Our readiness is essential to maximize the impact of this visitation.

The following briefly identifies and explains a revival cycle.

Revival. A visitation of God upon His people. Here the church more completely represents Christ in purity, power, and love than during non-revival seasons. When the church walks in these things, the world responds with a hunger for God. Conversions, in great numbers, are always the result.

Apathy. Apathy begins as a gradual decline in the fervency of the heart of believers for God. The blessings of the Lord become common and are considered optional. The passion, which hungers and thirsts after God, is replaced with ritual and tradition. And power gives way to form. Apathetic people still hold to spiritual values, but mostly as memories.

Compromise. What started as the failure to uphold the standards for right living, becomes the entrance for wrongdoing. Standards of righteousness decline, giving way to deception. Deception brings demonic chaos, resulting in sin as a lifestyle. Deception always comes through the door called compromise.

Sin. People openly embrace evil, calling it good. The righteous are mocked and the wicked are honored. With the fear of God all but vanished, humankind and pleasure are exalted as gods.

Bondage. Repeated sin gives legal access to the devil. And he never passes up an opportunity to afflict those who were created in God's image. God allows the enemy to come and oppress whenever His people give way to sin. Such allowances come from God's mercy. It's from the "pigpen" that some people best recall the provisions of the Father. From the place of bondage and oppression we learn how to pray again.

Prayer. This kind of praying is desperate and void of all religion. Through humiliation we begin to lose sight of all things that are temporal. We are reduced to the one thing that all true believers have in common—we are people who cry out to God and He hears us. God responds with mercy and vindicates us against our enemies.

REVIVAL—DIVINE VISITATION

The point to remember is not the actual cycle of revival. It's the point at which God visits His people again; the season of desperate prayer. All who hunger for Him are filled. No one is ever tuned away.

In the past 250 years there have been four revivals that actually changed the nations of the world. Today the prophets from the many "tribes" of the church agree—we are facing what should become the greatest revival in all history.

So how can we prepare for revival? It takes much more than studying revivals of the past. I remind you, the Pharisees were the revival experts of their day. Yet they missed Jesus when He came because He didn't come the way they expected. It also takes more than praying for revival. Even in that area we'd have to give the Pharisees top honors. They were known for much prayer. And certainly they prayed with the rest of Israel for the coming Messiah.

Our hunger for revival must go beyond our desire for a move of God. Revival is the result of us hungering for God Himself! His visitation, the outpouring of His Spirit, the release of great blessings, are all the result of the church taking Jesus as her First Love again. The issue of the day is not really revival. The real issue? It's time for a renewed passion for the Lover of our souls—Jesus, the Son of God. So stay simple in your devotion to Christ, keeping it practical with a love for the people of God—and invite the God of surprises to come anyway He wants. More Lord!

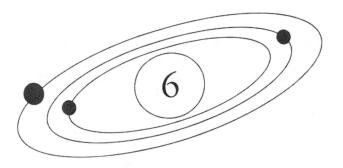

GOOD OR BEST?

It has often been said that the good is the greatest enemy of best. As Christians, the good that most often opposes us is religion (form without power, ritual without life). Religion focuses on doing good things but is motivated by a value for outward form rather than the impulse of the Spirit's life and power.

A common way many of us become religious is by a wrong response to the genuine leading of the Spirit. In any given situation, the Spirit will emphasize a particular truth or key to guide us through that situation and equip us with the principles of the Kingdom. But we are never to think that this one principle is the *key to life*. It seems every spiritual principle, whether deliverance, fasting, or a method of Bible study, is turned into a fad by a few people who think they're to build their entire life on practicing that one thing.

The only true key to life is your relationship with Christ. He modeled what it meant to choose the best in every situation by only doing what His Father was presently doing. For you to do only what *He* is presently doing, you need to maintain a continuous openness to His voice. When you make this connection with Him your main priority, you will be able to recognize the priority of the present moment in which you are living. The moment you are listening more to what He said yesterday than to what He is saying today, is the moment you start positioning yourself to miss that what He is saying is best. Consequently, you'll be doing something other than His will.

This is the primary thrust of the biblical story of the Good Samaritan. There we see a priest and a Levite on their way to a meeting to serve God. They each run directly into someone who is injured and in dire need of help. But they each choose the meeting because they think staying "clean" is more important than "Love your neighbor as yourself." They prioritized the details of the law over its life-giving purpose, and these upside-down priorities caused them to miss out on what God was doing.

I have been guilty of prioritizing a spiritual principle above attending to the present voice of the Spirit. When I first learned of the power and priority of *praise*, I wouldn't think of having any kind of gathering where we didn't honor God in this way. At that time I was responsible for organizing evangelistic concerts. Some of the greatest Christian artists in the country would come to these events. But before the artist would come out to minister, I would lead the group, many of whom were unbelievers coming to hear the gospel, in 30 to 40 minutes of worship and praise. Looking back, I see that I was actually forcing the praise to happen. I'm not saying it's wrong to lead praise and worship at an evangelistic event, but for me in those instances, it was. I was taking the principle to an extreme because I thought it was *the* key to life. As a result, the praise was actually more of a religious ritual than true spiritual worship.

The good is called the *enemy* of the best for a reason. If you have walked with Christ for any length of time, you know that staying focused on doing what Jesus is doing will cause conflict with the priorities of those around you. Years ago, one of our youth pastors took a team to Mexico to help build some buildings for an orphanage. There happened to be several other groups working at the same orphanage, and at one point another youth pastor approached ours and tried to set up some kind of meeting with the two youth groups. In order to do this, however, our youth group would have had to cut back on the hours they had committed to the building projects.

Our youth pastor told the man, "We're here to work." The man persisted, emphasizing the priority of unity between the teams. When our youth pastor repeated, "We're here to work," the man began to argue that the buildings they were working on would all be left to burn after Christ returned. Apparently, some people mistakenly think that physical work is not spiritual. Our pastor responded again in the same way, and the man finally went away frustrated. In keeping the commitment they'd made, our youth group grew in character, and the orphanage benefited from their hard work. The other group had much less success.

Earlier I said that we need to stay present with the Lord in order to recognize the priority of the moment. We each have a list of priorities that we are responsible to steward in our lives. When we honor what the Lord says is most important and stay current with His voice, then these other priorities can each be given their proper time and attention. There may be conflicts of interest that arise at times, but His voice gives us the wisdom we need to work them out. Without listening, these conflicts will always lead us to neglect certain priorities in the name of honoring others.

For example, a pastor has a priority to shepherd the church. The first church he must shepherd, however, is his own family. I believe and practice this principle. A pastor I knew had a more difficult time managing these two priorities. One Tuesday he missed a meeting he was supposed to attend. He had given no one notice that he would be gone, so someone called him later to tell him they'd missed him. He said, "My family is my priority, and I needed a night to be with them." Of course, no one could argue with that. But he failed to mention that the other nights of the week were filled with recreation and work appointments, leaving him with one night to choose between family or ministry responsibilities. He may have made the right choice in staying with his family that night, but it was only to remedy the poor choices he'd made that put them in the position of desperately needing him to be around as a husband and father. Most people would find no fault in his action. But when God called him to be a pastor, He gave him what he needed to fulfill all his responsibilities. The fact that he was having a hard time being responsible is a sign that he was probably letting the good get in the way of the best.

We all face the challenge of recognizing the responsibilities God has given us, but never letting them take the place of the main priority—doing what He is doing, and saying what He is saying. Our focus on Him, or our lack of focus, determines whether we will be successful at choosing the best, all the time.

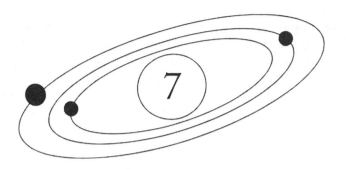

MY NEW DOG

A childhood dream became reality this past week. I was given a first-class hunting dog—a German Shorthair Pointer. He's only nine weeks old and has already shown his instinct for finding and retrieving game. Not only that, his first night in our house was incredible. He slept all night in the laundry room without barking or whining. When I first brought him into the house, I thought I might have heard him say, "I'm here to please you. Please show me where you'd like me to do my 'business' and I'll try to accommodate your every wish. And oh, by the way, I love little birdies to pieces." Since then I realize that I was just hearing things—he has backslidden completely. He sometimes forgets where to do his "business" and whines and barks very nicely, thank you very much. Oh well, we still love Rez (named after my favorite band).

Do you have a prayer list? I do. It's not always one that is on paper, but it's written on my heart in bold letters. I have often thought of my list as having both important and unimportant items. The important things have to do with human life and eternity. The unimportant can be material or even circumstantial. My question is, why would God bypass my important list, filled with spiritual priorities, and answer a desire that has nothing to do with anything that is obviously holy? The only answer I can come up with—because He wanted to.

Our heavenly Father is perfect in every way. There is no waste in Heaven's government. And in His perfect wisdom, He knew that it was more important for me to learn about His character as the Father than it was for me to have my "priority prayers" fulfilled. After all, I expect Him to care about the important things of my life. How refreshing it is to see that He cares about things that score very low on the Eternity Rating Chart, just because He loves me.

There once was a king named Cyrus. Isaiah prophesied about him, name and all, before he was ever born. One of the words that God spoke over this man was this: *"I will give you the treasures of darkness. . .so that you may know that it is I, the Lord, the God of Israel, who calls you by your name"* (Isa. 45:3 NASB). In this passage God promised to do many things for Cyrus. And not all of them would make our "priority" list. Yet God wanted this king to be fully convinced of his call in life, and who put him there. His plan was to reveal His hand of unusual provision and protection so that Cyrus would have branded forever in his own mind that he was there because of God's call.

I'd like to believe that it is very similar in our lives. God sometimes takes care of things that are not important just to remind us that He knows every desire and need that we have. And as our Father, His reach is so far that it even touches those things that have nothing to do with eternity. It seems to me that God simply wants to build our confidence in who He is and what He is like.

Unlike me, my dog has a confused master. We've had many dogs. I always figured that when the animal blows it, you spank him. If it's a mess he made, rub his nose in it, and put him outside. My confusion is this—the dog training manuals say not to do what I've always done.

I don't mind changing my ways, really. I'm just wondering if these trainers were raised by Dr. Spock. If you'll remember, in the '60s he told the nation that spanking was bad for children. And many listened (my parents weren't among them, however). He has since regretted his part in raising a generation of brats. I rejected Spock and his ideas simply because they go against the Bible. But what does the Bible say about raising my hunting dog? Until I find the answer to this puzzling question, I am, with reservation, going with the "experts." I just hope that I don't end up raising a pooch without principles.

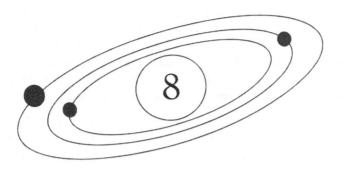

MUSTARD GREENS

God must laugh at some of the things we eat. He probably wonders, *How could they actually think that I created that to be eaten?* Mustard greens must fit into that category.

My one and only encounter with that weed came in 1973. (I only remember important dates.) Beni and I were newly married and serving as volunteers at a church in Cotati, California. Occasionally someone from this tiny fellowship would bring the vegetables they had grown to the church and make them available to anyone who wanted them. This happened to be during one of our several seasons of trying to eat health foods. The announcement was made, "There are mustard greens on the back table. Help yourself." Anyone committed to eating health foods is brave by nature.

When no one took any of the greens, it should have given us our first clue that perhaps this time we should follow the crowd. We were Bible school students, which meant we were hungry. I weighed 30 pounds less than I did as a senior in high school when I was very lean from playing four sports! While eating healthy food was our goal, our greater priority was simply to eat. In fact, as a janitor, I used to eat the untouched food that was occasionally left by the workers in the offices that I cleaned (gross!). And day-old donuts and the like can't be considered health foods.

We proudly took our large bag of mustard greens with us as we returned home. We crammed it into the pressure cooker and did according to the book. How surprised we were when we opened the pot to find this little pile of greens, which looked suspiciously like spinach. (This should have been our second clue.) We sat down to the table for a delicious meal. After one bite we laughed and decided to fast.

That was the second time in our new marriage that I had considered, with food on the table, how good fasting looked. The other time was when we had enough money to buy a squash for dinner. My dictionary says squash means "to press into a flat mass or pulp." It seems to me that any food named after a violent act should fall into question. When I was growing up I liked all vegetables, if it was corn. My wife loves all vegetables, even the non-edible kinds like Brussels sprouts, lima beans, peas, etc. I don't think I had ever eaten squash until that moment. I tasted it and passed on any additional bites, hoping that someone had packed too much for lunch at the office I was about to clean.

The pressure of having little or nothing to eat was not such a big problem for us then. We were in love with Jesus, and He always took care of us although His timing was not always the same as ours. And we were in love with each other and just happy to be together.

Our appetites in life determine how we respond in a trial. I have since been in the same circumstances and have not handled the pressure of empty cupboards quite as graciously. But never has lack upset my spiritual apple cart when Jesus was really my First Love.

Pressure brings everything to the surface—the good, the bad, and the ugly. While I don't like it, pressure comes because of the mercy of God. Can you imagine what it would be like to live an entire life without seeing what was in our hearts through trial?

Many people turn their attention to how others have wronged them during their season of testing. That is one of the devil's better tricks. If I can be preoccupied with what's wrong with you, I'll never be in a place to see my own heart. If I can't see my heart, I can't repent and be changed. Let's face it, holiness—becoming like Jesus—is the purpose behind every trial.

The Kingdom of God is so different from everything else we know. Brokenness comes before healing. Weakness is the first step to strength. Seeing our hopeless condition is the prerequisite to experiencing His transforming power.

The sinner, who sees the depth of his sin and the calamity that it has caused, is less likely to ever return to that way of life. Jesus said, *"her sins, which are many, are forgiven, for she loved much"* (Luke 7:47). Is He saying that to love God you must sin a lot? No! No one loves the Father more than the Son, and He has never sinned! God is saying that the one who sinned a lot is more likely to be aware of their sin and their need for God. Love is the result of tasting such great forgiveness.

You've probably not wondered what reward the vegetable world will have in Heaven, but I have. If "the first will be last and the last will be first" applies to them too, I expect that mustard greens will become like good chocolate in Heaven. After all, being at the bottom of the totem pole of the vegetable world, you have nowhere to go but up. I also hear that lima beans have the inside track on being Heaven's raspberries.

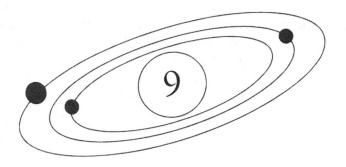

PLANNING

It is said that *when we fail to plan, we plan to fail*. I believe this. I am always planning something. In a simple drive down the road I'm planning on which car to pass and what lane to be in for the next move I'll make a half-mile away. Planning is necessary for that *battleground*.

I used this principle in all the planning that went into buying my sons their first pocketknives. Every young man needs a knife. And it must be written somewhere that dads are responsible for this purchase. That's because God knew that most moms wouldn't do it, especially for sons at the ages of 6 and 4.

I've never been into buying cheap stuff, especially with outdoor gear. If a knife is cheap, it won't get sharp. And if it won't get sharp, it's too easy to cut yourself. With a dull knife you work harder to cut something, exerting more effort, usually being careless. In doing so, you are much more likely to slip and rearrange the location or condition of certain body parts.

The brand that I chose was not as expensive as fine cutlery goes. But it would hold a good edge. Plus, it had one tremendous benefit—a guarantee. It said that if we break or *even lose* the knife, they would replace it for free. Remember, I was buying them for my boys. Even though they couldn't use them without our supervision, I knew it was very possible for these tools to mysteriously disappear.

They did lose them, just as I had planned. And the factory guarantee only proved that my purchase was a smart one. However, with all the planning, I forgot where I put the guarantee. It was only one step short of a *great* plan.

Every time I backpack into the Trinity Alps I think, *Why don't I come up here more often? It's in my backyard.* When I'm up there with my family, fishing and taking in the sights, the subject frequently comes up about next year's vacation. Our conclusion usually has us planning to spend more time in the Alps. Everyone agrees. When next year comes, we're busy, distracted, and a far cry from where we were when we decided to hike more often. If the truth were known, it is probably the hike into the high country that we remember most when we are not there. When we finally overcome distractions and actually pack into the Alps, we kick ourselves for waiting so long...just like last year.

On one such trip, I hiked in with my brother and my dad. We could only stay two days and one night. It was deer hunting season, so I thought I'd bring my bow just in case I ran into a deer that had received a Kavorkian's (the suicide doctor) gift certificate for one office visit. It didn't. But more importantly, I wanted to fish the evening hatch of mayflies in this little secluded lake where we were to camp.

Following our two-hour drive, we started the four-mile hike. It went well. Picture this—a father and two sons, all proving how manly they are and what incredibly good shape they're in. It started what was more like a gentleman's race to the lake, trying not to sweat or breathe hard. Trips like this can only happen with good planning. And since we were on my turf, I planned it all.

Along with my bow, I included my fishing rod, vest, and the two zillion flies that would probably all be needed. Several years earlier I made such a trip and discovered how important it is to have a tube in which to place my rod for protection. Charlie made one for me from PVC pipe. It doubled as a walking stick.

The hike in was our quickest to date. Since there were no kamikaze deer to be seen, I anxiously opened my rod case to pursue the high mountain brook and rainbow trout. When I opened the case, I found that I was one step short of a great plan, again. There was no rod in the case. Please don't misunderstand me; it's not that I don't enjoy the scenery. It's not that just being in that paradise doesn't do something for me. It's just that when trout are rising to bugs on the surface of the water, my arm starts to twitch. I have this uncontrollable urge to cast a fly. And I was a four-mile hike and a two-hour drive from my rod. So much for fishing.

God spoke to Israel saying, *"I know the plans that I have for you...plans for your welfare and not for calamity, to give you a future and a hope"* (Jer. 29:11 NASB). God's plans are for good. They are complete, positive, and designed with eternity in mind. And thankfully, He will not change His mind.

Consider this: Jesus came to die. That was the plan. The devil offered him the kingdoms of the world in order to distract Him from the plan. The people were ready to vote Him in as King, which would also nullify His intent. His own heart struggled with the fact that for the only time in all of eternity, He would be separated from the Father. He prayed, *"Take this cup away from Me; nevertheless not My will but Yours be done"* (Luke 22:42). Had He insisted on this desire, it would have canceled The Plan. But He didn't!

How many times have we given Him every right to stray from His desire for our welfare, to give us a future and a hope? But He is never one step short of a great plan. All His plans for us are great and complete! And according to Philippians 1:6, *"He who has begun a good work in you will complete it. . . ."*

I have a number of plans that I'm working on. They're good ones, too. If I can just remember where I put the guarantee and not get distracted, the plans will be fulfilled. . . to the glory of God.

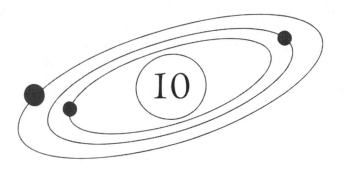

RAISING DOGS

How do you raise a dog? I thought I knew. We have had several dogs through the years, and they all seemed to turn out fine.

Maggie was our Irish setter. We got the pick of the litter of true championship stock. She would come when I called her. She would sit at my command, heel (a true Pentecostal) when we took a walk, and stay wherever I told her to stay as long as I wanted. Maggie seemed to want to obey. And like all our dogs, she was a house dog. Looking back, with hindsight the way it is, that dog was almost angelic in a dog sort of way. Shortly after our move to Weaverville, Maggie died a sad and premature death.

We've always preferred longhaired dogs, so a Cocker Spaniel seemed like our next logical choice. A friend of my aunt raised them and always gave away one of every litter. When they heard about our Maggie's death, they gave us a pup. We named her Corban, which is a biblical word meaning *gift*. Never mind about the fact that the word occasionally implied *a blood sacrifice*—Corban would live as a reminder that God concerns Himself with things that matter to us. She was His gift to us through some very considerate people.

I wish I could tell you about her great skills. She would come when we called her, if it was convenient. She would bark at other dogs, if we were present, and then would yelp, whine, and do the dog's version of a blood-curdling scream if that dog would so much as look at her the wrong way. She needed counseling, but wasn't open to it. When we discovered cancer throughout her body, we had the doctor cut it out. When it came back....

Leah, our chief pet lover, wanted another dog, badly. Through the generosity of Sharon Scroggins, we were able to give her a Shih Tzu, which she named Precious. (For those of you who are uneducated, a Shih Tzu is a small bundle of fur, with over-sensitive emotions.) She was the hardest dog for us to train. She was very much afraid of me. Once while the family was away, it actually jumped into another car, just to get away from me. The woman driver laughed. I was embarrassed; I'm sure I must have appeared to be a dog abuser. And I wasn't. Precious has never really learned much beyond her name, and "Go see Leah." Yet all we really require of her is to be *precious* for Leah. She is.

Please notice that we appear to be going downhill in our ability to *raise up a dog in the way he should go.* And the next addition to our lives seems to confirm that fact—Rez. Rez is my dog. My first dog, really. I love my dog. It's probably only puppy love, but it's what has sustained this short relationship to date. As mentioned previously, Rez is a German Shorthair. Imagine a toddler in Mike Tyson's body. That's my dog. He's not destructive by nature; he just destroys a lot. He has more energy than should be legal. When the Galvans watched him for the better part of a day, they discovered how mellow their own dog was—a Springer Spaniel, which they previously thought to be hyper. When I found out that Rez threw up on their floor, I asked if it was something he ate. They said yes; it was part of their couch. He must love couches; he ate part of mine, too. They came to church the next day just to repent for what they thought about me.

I had hoped that when I got Rez, I would learn a lot about dogs. I haven't. The lessons have been mostly about me. And the news isn't good. The day he tore up our linoleum floor in our laundry room was a day of great awakening. It was the flooring we had just laid when we remodeled the house. Rez almost went to meet Jesus. Instead of taking it out on him though, I just got bitter. As silly as it may sound to some, I had to repent and forgive. Bitterness shouldn't reside in us, regardless of who or what it's aimed at.

This past week I took Rez to a professional trainer. This man is also the breeder and is known for training pointers for hunting. That is what this dog was bred for—pointing at and retrieving game. Carlos drove with me. *Hmmm. . .is it because my dog ate his couch, and he wanted to see him punished?* We had a pleasant trip. I didn't want to put my wonderful dog in a cage for the five-hour drive, so I let him sleep in the back of the Isuzu Trooper. A cage seemed cruel. I was soon to discover that the car I wanted to sell now needed new carpet for the back. Rez tore it to shreds. *How could he do that with me in the car?* I don't know. But if you know of someone with a kennel for an SUV, cheap, let me know.

Driving onto the game preserve where we were to meet Dick, the trainer, we saw many pheasants. When Rez saw them, it was like a moment of revelation. He discovered his gift—the purpose for which he was born. He then tried to jump through the window; he scratched at the window, ran back and forth in the vehicle, and barked. He just plain lost what little composure he had previous to these sightings. As annoying as it might have been, I was encouraged. He is aggressive and birdy. To get something done in the field, you need an animal that loves what he's doing enough to endure affliction, bad weather, odd hours, etc.

The people that get the most done in the Kingdom are very similar to Rez. They have high energy, love what they do, endure affliction, bad hours, and less than convenient circumstances. They sometimes even destroy things—like stepping on the toes of the idle. In fact, come to think of it, they *usually* destroy things; it seems to come with the turf. But we all know that if you need something done, call them—they're dependable. If I could get my dog's anointing, without his insatiable drive to chew, I would use it, and pass it on to all I know. Imagine people loving what they do enough to endure affliction and anything else, all just to fulfill the purpose for which they have been born—to glorify God and make Him known.

When we left, Rez was in the dog kennel on the back of Dick's truck; he looked sad and abandoned. Carlos asked me if I would miss him. Thinking about Rez eating my wife's glasses, destroying my couch, my linoleum, the SUV carpet, and basically tie-dying our living room rug, I said, "No, he deserves it." I'm still working on my attitude.

I hope that when he's through being trained, I can start to learn about dogs. I'm sick of the present subject.

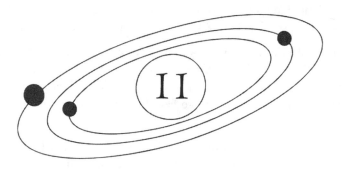

STRESS AND REST

Golf is near the top of the list of things I don't do well. I think it was Mark Twain who described golf as "one way to ruin a good walk." That makes sense to me. Even though I stink at the game, I have an attitude when I play. Whenever I come to a water hazard, I select my best ball from the bag. It's like I dare the pond to take my ball. If I pick a bad ball because I fear I might lose it in the water, I figure it's lost before I swing. This technique probably hasn't saved me many balls, but it makes my approach to the game more consistent with the way I think about the rest of life—no fear!

I've never been too moved or impressed with those who crumble under pressure. Pastors quit because they are under stress, marriages break up because of such pressure, and many fall into different sorts of evil, all with stress receiving the blame. When someone has said that they've been under a lot of stress, I've thought in my heart, *Who hasn't? What's the big deal?* It's not that I've been uncaring for those under pressure (especially if they are young in the Lord). I serve them the best I know how. It's just that I know from experience that stress has never been removed because I moaned it away. The one thing I've generally been able to do through the years is keep my perspective regardless of pressure. I know it is a gift from God to be able to do this—at least I know it now.

No one likes stress. Most of us cross the street when we see it coming. Yet I try to use stress for my advantage. In a weird sort of way, it has been a friend to me. It's what helped me to prepare for a test in school. In sports, it helped me to ignore pain and injury in hopes of a win. As a child of God, it has driven me to my knees...the altar of divine romance.

I said all that to say this: of late, I have been under quite a bit of stress. Impressed? Me neither. But my problem is, I've not handled it with the grace that I expect from a man of God. In my heart I know that it comes down to trusting God. That's what makes this whole situation so frustrating. I'm weak where I'm supposed to be strong.

I hide things like this pretty well—except from my wife. And even there, I try. This stress thing has affected my health. God created us to trust Him completely. Anything outside of trust puts us in conflict with nature. And that includes our physical bodies. Beni has been concerned...and secretly so have I. It looks like this water hazard got the best of me.

My wife picked me up from the office Thursday afternoon. I was anxious to get home, rest for a bit, and get back to the office for our worship team practice. I love to spend practice time with the musicians. I was already anticipating our Friday prayer meetings, especially the one at 10 P.M.—my favorite activity of the week for the past 15 years. As we approached our road, she didn't slow down. Sarcastically I said, "I live down there," pointing in the direction of our home.

She said, "We're not going home." I treasure every moment at home, so I prefer her to take me there before running other errands.

So I asked her with a slight, but indiscernible attitude, "Where are we going?"

She said, "Santa Cruz."

"No, where are we going?" I asked again.

Her smiling response was, "Santa Cruz."

"No, you can't do this to me," I said, as one who always handles surprises well. She insisted, so I did what every good husband would do...I grabbed the steering wheel, and helped her pull to the side of the road so we could talk. For me, spontaneity is *planning* to go somewhere new. And when I'm living on the wild side, I might even smile for no apparent reason.

After only a few moments it became apparent that she had all major bases covered and that she would not take to heart any of my brilliant reasons for staying. When she ran back to get our things hidden in the trunk, I resigned myself to go. Don't get me wrong—I love going to Santa Cruz, visiting my parents, and doing nothing significant. And I'm a far cry from a workaholic. I just have to be psyched up to miss a Friday night prayer meeting and a Sunday morning service. I had been kidnapped. It was a conspiracy to get me to rest. And after a near cardiac from the surprise, I did.

I was to discover that my parents had known of the conspiracy for two weeks. When we walked into the house, we were greeted with hugs from Mom and Dad and the television playing a taped copy of the 49ers' victory over Dallas from the previous week. Confirmation! I knew then, for sure, that this kidnapping was of God. The 49ers, the victorious 49ers, were there to greet me. With a fresh cup of French Roast, Dad and I watched the game again, along with the pre-game and post-game analysis, as well as the multitude of interviews. We played armchair quarterback, making decisions that would ensure a Super Bowl victory. It was glorious!

Stress is common. It's even been known to kill. But thankfully, that's unnecessary. Laughter remains a good medicine. Fellowship is still a powerful healing agent. And returning to the simplicity of devotion to Jesus is still the best way to refocus on His priorities. This whole process, that is unfinished, has me searching through my bag for the best ball. According to Scripture, my best ball is weakness with spiritual hunger. In my weakness His strength is seen for what it is—His ability triumphing over my inability, while He pours life into this needy, hungry soul.

I'm learning to get out of the water hazard—divine romance, fueled by simple devotion, ignited by coals from His altar. Need a light?

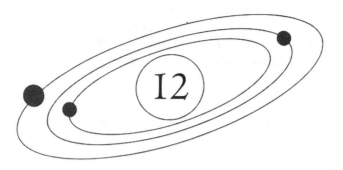

UNSTRINGING OUR BOW

Did you know that coffee was discovered by a goat herder? Apparently he noticed that his goats were jumping and running about with an unusual fervor. Upon further investigation he observed them eating a little bean that grew on local bushes. That was about A.D. 850. He desired to tap that source of energy for himself, and today it's called coffee.

The stories on the history of coffee are interesting, and some quite humorous. Childless women drank it in hopes of conceiving. And yet men drank it in great amounts, wanting to become less fertile. In 1657, the *Publick Adviser* ran an advertisement that said, "a very wholsom and Physical drink, having many excellent virtues, closes the Orifice of the Stomach, fortifies the heat within, helpth the Digestion, quickneth the Spirits, maketh the hearth lightsome, is good against Eye-sores, Coughs or Colds, Rhumes, Consumptions, Head-ach, Dropsie, Gout, Scurvy, King's Evil and many others...." (I don't have a clue about what most of that stuff is, which could signify that it worked as well as they said it should. By the way, I can't convince my spell checker that this is legitimate Old English.)

In 1911, Dr. Jonathan Hutchinson said that coffee "prevents headaches and fits the brain for work, that tea and coffee preserve the teeth, keep them in place, strengthen the vocal chords and prevent sore throat...have right to rank as nerve nutrient."

My favorite story has to do with Pope Clement VIII. It seems that there was a group in the church that wanted the Pope to declare coffee as a forbidden drink for believers. The Pope wisely asked for a taste. When he drank it, he declared, "Excellent!" He then went on to state that it would be tragic to assign such a great drink for infidels only. Then to relieve it of any possible evil, he "baptized" it! I do that daily. I *immerse* mine in near-boiling water.

I was raised to appreciate the finer things in life, at least the kind that most anyone could afford. I grew up hearing my grandfather say over and over again in his native Norwegian tongue, "Coffee is the best drink in the world." I'm so thankful for such a rich heritage. (I wonder if Pope Clement VIII was a relative?)

You might ask, "Where does one find such nonsense? After all, studying history was never so educating." One of the books in my library, *The Human Side of History*, from Mankind Publishing Company, deals exclusively with the manners and customs of people. When I picked it up last night to do some reading, my wife said that she was glad. Puzzled, I asked why. She mentioned something about me needing a *non-tense* book. Me, tense? What does she know?

Whatever our personal tendency is, being tense or mellow, we usually need occasional input from the opposite type of book or friend to stay spiritually healthy. Some people are so relaxed that they need a cattle prod permanently embedded in their posterior. Any passerby could bring some excitement to their day by pushing the right button. I'd even volunteer to "bless" them myself. There are others who are the essence of serious. They exhaust me. I have to psych myself up just to say "hi" to them. After all, how could "hi" ever be enough with so many problems in the world? And everyone knows that it's been left up to the two of us to solve them all ourselves, today. How's the weather? They don't have a clue!

Bob Mumford calls this need "unstringing our bow." If an archer leaves his re-curve bow strung, it will actually lose strength. It becomes accustomed to its bent position and has less will to send the arrow forth forcefully when a shot is attempted. In the same way, the overly tense person loses their effectiveness for the times when intensity without distraction is needed most. This kind of individual must be able to rest, laugh at himself, and keep all of life in a healthy perspective.

On the other hand, the carefree type needs to be able to weep and labor in sacrificial service on behalf of those who are well-acquainted with the trials of life. It would do them well to travel a bit and see how the rest of the world lives. Their heartstrings must be tugged now and then to be certain that they're still alive—hopefully more "now" than "then"!

My wife was honestly glad that I picked up that crazy history book. It would provide something not-so-intense for me to enjoy. Why do I need that? Apparently I've been a little too stern of late. I usually get that way when I take myself too seriously. And she does a good job helping me to remember the parts of life that are not so *life and death*.

If my wife had read my book first, she probably would have suggested that I just go and get another cup of coffee. After all, coffee "maketh the heart lightsom." And I've been saying that for years.

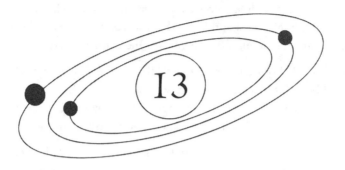

WRITING LETTERS

My grandpa came from the generation that wrote letters to stay in touch with loved ones. My generation makes phone calls. It's so much easier. Yet, I remember him reading and rereading each letter. I'm so busy that writing a letter just slows me down too much. Not only do you have to slow down to write a good letter, you have to think. Neither activity suits me well.

If we were to walk into the room when Grandma or Grandpa was reading a letter, we would hear how Aunt Agnes was doing, even if we didn't have a clue who she was. The letters were kept in a box. You never knew when you might need to read them again.

There is one area that I fail in as a friend and good relative more than any other— writing letters. One of my problems is that it does slow me down. But the greater problem is that it takes me too long to write. I treat each letter as though it were the Great American Novel. Unfortunately, if you were to read one, you wouldn't be able to see the amount of effort that I put into writing it. If it showed, it might be worth the time.

Some say that it's this perfectionism thing in me. It can't be that. But I do remember my dad receiving a letter from a fellow pastor. In it were all kinds of mistakes, with words crossed out and handwritten words in their place. It came from a large church. My dad took it to his secretary and told her, "Please don't ever send out a letter like this." He was right, and I work to carry the torch of *excellence*. (I think that is a much nicer word than *pickiness* or *vanity*.)

I know that on one occasion I offended one of our office workers. She was cutting the edges off of a little booklet that we were publishing. She was cutting them crookedly. I admit, it was only slightly crooked. I also admit that probably nobody else on the planet would have noticed. And if they did, they wouldn't have cared. But I did. So I showed her how to cut it straight. She didn't receive my instructions too well (you learn to discern these things after awhile), and later told me that I had better things to do with my time... like pastoring. I probably should have spent the time writing letters.

My list of people I owe a letter to is large. It is overwhelming to me. Someone in my position would be able to handle this load with no problem. If you have a problem like I do, I can give you good counsel. If you respond to the counsel, you will do better and conquer the *letter writer's block.* I only wish I knew how to follow my own counsel.

I'm learning though...ever so slowly. I pick at my list, little by little, sending out inferior material. My image of excellence is crashing, but at least a few of my friends are hearing from me.

It's probably good that the telephone wasn't invented during the apostle Paul's day. We might not have any epistles to read. Just big phone bills.

I called a good friend the other day. He had a phone number that I needed. When I called he said, "What do you want?" I said, "What do you mean, what do I want?" So he proceeded to tell me that the only time I call him is when I want something. (I realize that the tone of what I just wrote sounds rude. It was much more humorous than rude...but that is difficult to convey on paper.)

I acted like he was totally out of line for even suggesting that I had called him for any other reason than just to see how he was doing. And then, I was saved by the bell. He had another call and promised to return mine as soon as he was finished. During that time I scrambled to find that phone number. I even called information in Georgia...bingo! I got the number. Now I was actually positioned to talk on the phone, inquire how he was doing, and not ask for anything. I figured I'd come out smelling like a rose, or at least a true friend. He called back. I enjoyed my *smell,* but only for a moment. I had to admit and confess to him that I had called to get a phone number.

You see, I am also bad at phone calls. I used to have my sister make my phone calls for me in my youth. She didn't like making the calls. But threats from her *strong and brave* older brother seemed to help, sometimes. Today my wife helps me...if I've been good.

If I were the apostle Paul, not only would there be *no* Epistles, no one would have received many phone calls, either. But there *would* be good-looking booklets with nice, even edges.

Sometimes I spend an hour on something that has very little value, only to be left with just a few minutes to work on something that is very important. Perhaps my booklets versus letters dilemma would work to illustrate this point. People are God's priority. Anything that directly affects their lives is important. Anything that mostly affects my appearance before them isn't.

The psalmist prayed, *"Teach us to number our days, that we might present to you a heart of wisdom"* (Ps. 90:12 NASB). This verse tells me to do more than acknowledge that I won't live on this planet forever. It also seems to urge me to use the time that I have wisely. I think I'll go write a letter...maybe even a sloppy one.

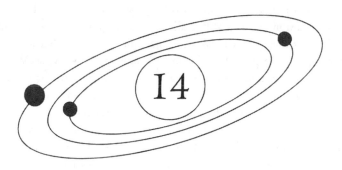

Rez Is Coming Home

I have a dog—a very famous dog. Some dogs reach fame by saving those caught in an avalanche or finding someone trapped under the rubble of an earthquake. Others reach that pinnacle in *dog-dom* through unusual loyalty to their master. And even others get the big break and make it to Hollywood, starring in movies and television sitcoms. After all, even a puppet named Alf made it at one time. All it takes is a good manager, talent, and excellent timing.

My dog, however, did none of these things. My dog is famous because he lived. He's a true survivalist. Yes, I'm referring to Rez, named after my favorite band, if you recall, the Rez Band—formally called The Resurrection Band. Bummer—I doubt they are flattered.

Rez is lucky to be alive. He never should have made it to six months of age. With all the damage that he did to our home, household goods and basic mental health, he's truly lucky to be alive. Most owners would have snapped, abandoning all rhyme and reason, and shot the dog. I've had more than one person basically volunteer to be the hit man— true friends helping friends in need. I ignored them because of my loyalty to the dog.

Have you ever owned a car that you *poured* money into, repairing everything in it that moved, and a few items that didn't? I've had one of those, too! After the umpteenth repair you think, *What else could go wrong? We could never recover our investment.* So you decide to keep it. After all, it's almost a brand-new car by now. And then, *what else could go wrong* was discovered. So it has been with Rez. The linoleum, the carpet, the silk plants, our couch (and the Galvans' couch), the carpet in our SUV, not to mention the immeasurable damage to my nerves, all destroyed in part by a German Shorthair named Rez.

Note: Now, all of this is so I can enjoy hunting with my sons. Hunters, you understand. Little explanation is needed. But all you anti-hunters, be not offended. Instead, you should rejoice, realizing that for most of us, hunting is a costly endeavor, and that it probably shortens our lifespan. And the animals almost always win. Occasionally some poor unsuspecting critter, unusually genetically inferior, dies of old age at the same millisecond that our guns go off, just to humor us in the insane pursuit of animals with greater instincts than we have intelligence. Rez is the ultimate preparation for such a futile quest. I also think that it could be said that there are many anti-hunters who would have changed their position on hunting had they been the owner of Rez. But even so, I doubt that they ever would have become accustomed to eating German Shorthair.

Shortly after I sent him to the trainers, he contracted the dreaded Parvo disease. Most dogs die from that one. The vet said there wasn't much hope. But he lived. Why? God is not through with me yet.

His strict training schedule was reinstated, and he got very sick again. How? This time it was because he ate a dead skunk. And that was the straw that broke the camel's back. Dick the trainer told me, "I've never seen anything like it. He'll eat anything!" I just smiled, assuring him that I understood. He then told me that he now remembers my dog as a pup. Rez used to climb into the food dish and growl at his brothers and sisters who would come to eat. When he was finished he'd allow the others to eat. Why doesn't this surprise me? Dick then promised he'd break him of the *eat anything* trait. (How is it that I, who cannot presently eat a ripe banana because of the pain caused by my braces, own a dog that will eat anything that's not walking? And I'm not even sure he wouldn't attempt it if it were moving in an appetizing sort of way.)

Rez is ready to come home. One could say that he's had a conversion of sorts, although I have yet to see the fruit of his *repentance*. I hope to soon. July is now slated as the time of his homecoming.

I have mixed emotions. Life has been so peaceful without him. It's been five months. We've all calmed down. Leah's dog, Precious, has had her own rebirth, coming out of her, "I'm an old grouch" attitude that she picked up when Rez became part of the family.

On the one hand, my dog is coming home. On the other, "my brothers and sisters, whenever you face trials of any kind, consider it nothing but joy" is coming home. Wow! I never thought of it that way. My joy-builder is coming home—either by fun, or by trial, joy. Trial tests faith and tested faith builds endurance and endurance that is allowed to have its full effect makes us mature and complete, lacking in nothing. God must really love me. He's provided a sure-fire way to joy, if I'll cooperate. And I think I will.

SIMPLE LIFE

I read a statement from Bill Gothard this past week that defines *contentment:* "If I am not satisfied with what I have, I will never be satisfied with what I want." Being Christians in a materialistic world, we sometimes get caught in the crossfire of conflicting lifestyles. Most of us can repeat the sermons on a simple life but struggle with daily pressures to have what humankind has lived without for centuries. Possessing has never been a problem biblically. It's being possessed by things that creates the conflict.

I've been thinking recently about the term "simple life." Why is it that my nature is to make the Christian life more difficult than it is? Maybe it's so that when I struggle, I'll feel justified by the degree of stress I feel. Who knows?

There is a secular book released recently whose title has evoked many curious thoughts: *Everything I Need to Know About Life I Learned in Kindergarten* by Robert Fulghum. It repeats some of those simple lessons—Don't take something that belongs to someone else, share your toys with others, don't fight, etc. Can you imagine a world where people live like that? To quote Bob Dylan, "When He returns."

There are many things that I don't understand in the Bible. But to be honest, I have a greater challenge with what I understand. For example, Jesus never said to give until it hurts. He said to give it all. It's that simple. And the power that we pray for is found in such simplicity.

The simple life is not necessarily one of few possessions. There are many poor people who do not enjoy the supposed liberty that is to be found in that kind of simple life. No, it's not found in quantity. It's found in quality. This is determined by our focus. Another term is devotion—complete, total devotion. That's the simple life. And giving is the natural expression of that devotion.

And old hymn by Judson W. Van DeVenter says, "All to Jesus I surrender, all to Him I freely give. I will ever love and trust Him, in His presence daily live. I surrender all, I surrender all. All to thee, my blessed Savior, I surrender all."

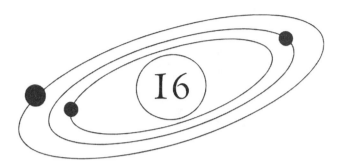

LAUGH

We had a wonderful ministers' meeting this past week. It was another time when we were able to speak into each others' lives. To do so, there must be openness and humility, as well as trust. God is building those elements into the spiritual leaders of this community. I am very thankful to witness and experience that work of grace.

One of the things that we discussed was the need to "unstring our bow." As pastors, we are sometimes the guiltiest of being too intense, all the time. There is certainly a time for that determined approach to life. But if there is no reprieve, it kills everyone around us. It's not healthy.

A bow that is always strung loses its strength. Anyone, pastor or not, will lose strength by living constantly "on the edge." Our bodies react to that kind of life with ulcers, high blood pressure, etc. Perhaps this is why the Bible teaches us that *"laughter is good medicine"* (see Prov. 17:22).

One of the hardest things to do is to laugh at ourselves. Yet it probably holds the strongest "medicine." Maybe our funny bone is tickled when we see our attempt to be more spiritually mature than we really are. Or maybe it's when we see ourselves try to out-guess God. Most of us have these experiences, but few receive their full medicinal value.

One of the most hilarious seasons in our life was before conversion. Stop and think about the excuses we made up to stay away from church, or God. (Of course, it's only funny this side of repentance.) And then there are the many blunders and embarrassing moments.

Laugh. Take time to share funny moments with others. Laugh together. And by all means, be real. Summer was never meant to be a time of retreat. It is a wonderful time to "unstring your bow." Have a hilarious summer!

THE WINDS OF CHANGE

I've told you before that for the past seven years plus, I've eaten the same breakfast almost every Sunday morning—biscuits and gravy. If the Brewery Restaurant is closed for spring-cleaning, or I'm out of town, it throws me off of my routine. My wife, on the other hand, doesn't like the thought of eating the same thing twice in a row (or even at the same location), let alone week after week for years. From my perspective, I found what I like—why change? But her point of view is that variety is to be experienced and enjoyed. From a church history perspective, she would adapt to the winds of change more easily than I. I, without God's grace, would tend to stay with whatever is more convenient and comfortable.

The winds of change are blowing. God is dealing with His church and is bringing about transformation. It is good and not a moment too late.

Winds of Change (written in the early '90s):

Germany has become one nation.

The Soviet Union hasn't.

The hostage takers of 1979 (Iran) became the hostage deliverers of the '90s.

Parents may be able to place their children in the school of their choice, if the voucher ($2,500 each) passes in the next election.

The Assemblies of God (our denominational affiliation) is going through a restructuring process at the district office.

Mountain Chapel (us) is going through a restructuring process.

But perhaps the most earth-shattering of them all—I am involved in two things I thought I would never do—lifting weights and learning how to use the computer.

And now we know that *anything* is possible.

Many are restless in a time of change. And there are those who know their "Rock." *"When my heart is overwhelmed, lead me to the Rock that is higher than I"* (Ps. 61:2).

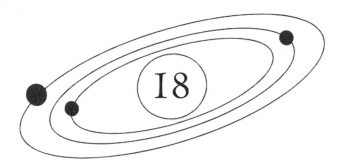

EXPLOSIVE UNDER PRESSURE

A friend of mine visited the Redwoods some years ago. His guide was explaining how the rings of a tree trunk reveal the age of that tree. These trees were hundreds of years old, and some even a couple thousand. As they examined one particular stump, they noticed two rings that were very large. When the forestry official was asked about it, he explained that one ring was from the 1886 drought and the other was during a heavy infestation of beetles that threatened the life of the forest in the 1920s (I don't remember the exact years). God has put it within nature that the greatest strength for survival is during the time of greatest pressure—this tree actually grew at an extraordinary rate during those two times.

A phrase from the back of a can of spray paint comes to mind—"Flammable! Dangerous when exposed to extreme pressure." That should be written on the forehead of every Christian and on the door of every church. "I am extremely flammable by the Spirit of God. And I am the most dangerous to the kingdom of darkness when under pressure."

I like Mario Murillo's statement, "I'm the evangelist the devil warned you about." Dangerous. Flammable. Explosive. All because of heat and pressure. James put it this way in James 1:2-3 (NASB): *"Consider it all joy when you encounter various trials, knowing that the testing of your faith produces endurance."* Pressure produces! It reveals the cracks in our faith, and at the same time displays the faithfulness of God—over and over again.

The Body of Christ has faced a greater pressure in the past three years than in any time I know. The good news is that we are extremely flammable—ready to explode in revival.

DROUGHT VERSUS WINTER

We left the sunny Bahamas this past Monday morning. That night we found ourselves driving home through this year's first snowstorm. What a contrast! Sunning ourselves by the cruise ship's pool one day and driving through a blizzard the next. What a life!

When I got up the next morning, I was surprised to see so many trees (some 30 and 40 years old) that had fallen from the storm. Limbs were scattered, power lines were down, and work crews were doing their best to clean up the damage caused by only 6 to 8 inches of snow. Was this the biggest storm of the past 30 years? No way! The major difference between this storm and the others was that this one followed six years of drought.

During one of the week's prayer meetings, it was pointed out that some of the trees that were destroyed wouldn't have been had they been pruned. It was also mentioned that one particular tree was damaged by the storm because of an unusual amount of leaves that were still on the tree—unusual because other trees of its kind shed their leaves quite awhile ago. And by the tree not ridding itself of its foliage, its leaves worked as a net, catching the snow until it became too heavy, and the branches broke.

The lessons from these events in nature are easy to translate into our lives. 1) Drought prepares us for failure. Is that fair? Yes, because drought is unnecessary. Jeremiah told us that the man who trusts in God is planted by a stream and is always bearing fruit— drought proof! The issue is trust. 2) Pruning (discipline) is good—not fun, but good. In this illustration, it's evident that being corrected by God enables us to stand strong in a storm. Without discipline, all growth is suspect! The issue is submission to God's purposes in using whatever He desires to make us more like Jesus. 3) We must know the seasons in which we live. King David fell into immorality because in the season of war, he was looking for a woman. Not only did he find a woman, he found a war that he was not prepared to win. And he failed. Following the Holy Spirit daily assures us of being in tune to the seasons. The issue is our awareness of God's presence and our willingness to follow (abiding in Christ).

There is a difference between winter and drought. Winter is a time of God's correction and renewal for the coming season of growth. Drought is marked with indifference, apathy, and hopelessness, and it is without a living vision.

It is comforting to know that while I can't put an end to winter, I can put an end to drought.

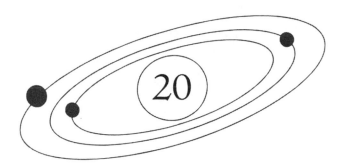

NEVER AGAIN

I, Bill Johnson, being of a reasonably sound mind, do hereby solemnly swear that I will never again have a tooth pulled while being awake. I promise!

I should have known better too, especially when I saw the nurses' faces after telling them that they were to give me a "local." They had that look that said, "You poor thing." But being a good steward and wanting to save a buck, I stood unwavering, undaunted, and bravely climbed into the chair.

For me to write in detail what happened in the following moments would require a PG-13 rating on this week's bulletin. But suffice it to say, it was war. The tooth broke, leaving the three roots firmly impacted. The doctor went after them like Ronnie Lott on a blitz to an unprotected quarterback. Even the Three Stooges would have been inspired with fresh ideas for a new film clip. My grip on the armrests must have been similar to a civilian's first ride on an F-14 fighter jet. Only in my case, the grip was to keep me from becoming airborne. And it was all to save a few dollars.

It's not that all my financial choices have been bad. But I've spent when I should have saved. And I've saved when I should have spent. And only a good memory will keep this thing from happening again at the oral surgeon's office.

If we repeat the same mistakes over and over again, it's usually because we have forgotten the sting of yesterday's sin. Wisdom has a good memory. And for the one willing to learn from his or her mistakes, it can be said that there is no such thing as a bad investment—if there's a good memory.

I don't know the name of the drug used to put people to sleep, but today I'd almost be willing to buy stock in the company. They'll always have at least one faithful customer.

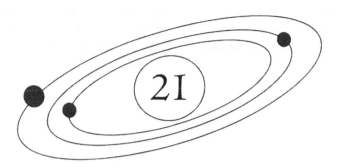

PAPER FOR FIRE

My dad once quoted a statement to me that was used when he went to Bible school: "It takes a little paper to get a fire going." It means that it is sometimes good for a pastor to use notes for his sermon. This past week I spoke at the women's meeting and taught on how to keep the flame burning in our hearts. The flame in this instance refers to zeal, hunger, life, etc. Paul taught Timothy that he was responsible to stir up the embers of his heart and keep them burning (see 2 Tim. 1:6-7).

It is sometimes difficult to explain things that you feel. But sitting here at my desk I began to experience an overwhelming sense of encouragement just by glancing at the books on my shelf. Why? Memories. As I look at one, I remember Jack Hayford relating the story of the church that he pastors. I am better off today because of that ministry in my life. In another I recall the joy of reading Tommy Reid's book, *Kingdom Now, But Not Yet,* and how I wish I had written it. Perhaps more accurately than any other that I've read, it communicates my heart. Testimonies of our own book, *Jennie,* and other great men and women of God remind me that "nothing is impossible with God" (see Luke 1:37).

That fire has been ignited in me over and over again as I proved that the fuel found the shelves of our Christian bookstores. This is the "information age." There is more at the disposal of the average American family today than probably that of 100 families just a century ago. The paper needed to start the fire of our souls is within arm's reach of everyone. Take advantage of the bounty to which we have access. The Bible tells us that His people "die for the lack of knowledge" (see Hos. 4:6). It's not that knowledge is unavailable; it's just not pursued. So pursue and enjoy.

On the downside, our own city's "No Other Name" bookstore will close its doors on Monday. Why? Not enough business to pay expenses. Thank you, Winnie, for providing a great service for the Christian community! This chapter is closed, for now.

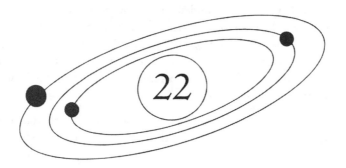

REMINDERS OF INNOCENCE

Bill Gothard has a wonderful series of books entitled *Character Sketches*. Each chapter is focused on one particular animal and how godly character can be learned from its example. In our house it became known as the "Two Animal Book," as each night I would read about two different animals to my children.

The pictures in *Character Sketches* are great. The lesson material is worth the attention of adults and children alike. Each chapter begins with a map outlining the domain of the animal being studied. I used that map to introduce my children to the nations of the world. In the days when they first learned to talk, they would point to India, or perhaps the continent of Africa or Greenland, at my request. I'll never forget the day I introduced them to Hong Kong. They laughed and laughed as though they were embarrassed for those who had to live in a place with such a funny-sounding name. And every time I would ask them to point to Hong Kong on the map, they would each look at the other, repeat the name "Hong Kong," and laugh. They never seemed to forget its location.

One of our family pastimes is to recall the humorous stories of our children growing up. If they're too embarrassing for them, we keep the stories for family only. We do it because it's fun. But it also seems to keep a child connected to the innocence of his or her past. Through this we are able to reinforce strong family ties by maintaining good memories.

I have a theory: Teenagers who have small children in their lives have a more realistic view of life than do those who are surrounded only by adults and peers. (This may be true for adults as well.) Infants stir up emotional instincts—like the drive to protect and care for somebody. With small children around, there is a greater awareness that our choices affect more than "just me."

Very few of us have babies around the house at the same time we have teenagers. Yet we can all make sure we associate with people who have small children, whether they be other Christians, neighbors, or relatives. Reviewing the wonder of their birth, confessing your incomprehensible joy over them, and reciting the great memories of their years of early childhood all work to reinforce a much-needed innocence for a healthy view of life.

When Leah was 2 years old, she put on her new dress and stood before the mirror. After examining herself thoroughly, she stated emphatically, "I sure do look pretty darn!" That phrase has stuck in my family for these many years now—a cute reminder of the impact of innocence.

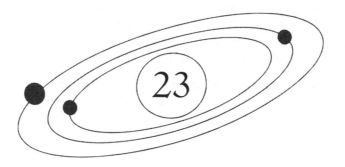

WRITING

For years now I have bought books on writing, hoping that someday I would actually be an author. Some of these books teach the reader how to write properly, covering the laws of grammar, sentence structure, and many other similar rules that I've not yet learned. Others try to inspire the reader to be creative. Usually they motivate through profound statements and sometimes even stories of the accomplishments of other noted individuals.

My favorite book on writing is *If You Want to Write* by Brenda Ueland. While this book is more on creativity in personal expression (any art form), it gives some instruction and a lot of inspiration. My greatest treasure from this author is the growing conviction that even I can write. She tackles the subject unlike anyone I have ever heard before. I wish that she could have been one of my schoolteachers.

Why would anyone want to be a writer? It is some of the most mentally demanding work that I've ever attempted. Few things can be as frustrating as a trash can full of thoughts that didn't gel. But then, golf comes pretty close.

I have had many a tense moment on the golf course. Golf demands perfection. There is only one goal—no matter how long it takes you, the ball must go in the hole. Writing has amazing similarities, including sand traps, water hazards, and many other roadblocks to success. But if you hit it well, and the goal is reached in reasonable time, it is a job well done.

My one motivation for writing is that I love to write. I was brain dead for most of my high school years. Grammar school wasn't much better. And if there was a subject that I liked, it wasn't English—for which I suffer today.

Yet my love for writing enables me to endure my own ignorance and motivates me to want to learn. It's the reason behind the hours of labor on a project that only a few people will read. It is the fire that seems to fight back when all indications are that I'll never be a good writer. Do I seek success? No, it's excellence I seek.

What do you love? Does it bring you pain? Have you risen above your fear of failure? Are you pursuing excellence to the point of sacrifice? I hope so. If not, find something else to love.

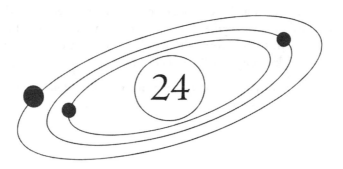

My New Toy

I'm getting a new toy. But it's not just any toy. Besides being packed with lots of fun, this one is a monument that points to God's faithfulness and the love of God's people. I'm hoping for its arrival today via UPS.

What is a monument in the Bible? It's a physical object that reminds us of a particular work of God. It also might speak of a specific characteristic of God or of a certain time period when God revealed His faithfulness in a personal way.

I wonder what my schoolteachers would say about my new toy? It was my fifth grade teacher who had to put up with my complaints about writing—"My hand gets too tired." My seventh grade teacher endured a written report that through the miracle of wide lettering I was able to stretch what was probably about a five-page report into the fourteen pages he required. In ninth grade I received an "F" for one quarter in spelling. When I was a junior in high school, my teacher, Miss McDougal, felt it best to take my whole class back to an eighth grade textbook to relearn grammar. I learned it well enough to ace the test. Unfortunately, most of it was forgotten soon afterward. And nearly all my teachers would say to my parents, "Billy could be such a good student if he wouldn't daydream so much." I wonder what they would think of my new toy.

Dreams have an unusual way of affecting our lives—not the dreams of the night, but the dreams of the heart. On many occasions I've told you of my aspirations to write. I didn't confess that to you because I wanted you to know. My confession came from the realization that if you knew what was in my heart, I'd be more likely to pursue it.

Several members of this body have encouraged me to pursue all that's in my heart. Their actions have followed their words. In this case, several of them pooled their resources to help me buy a new toy—an Apple Powerbook (laptop computer). And to them goes the spoil. For as I write and people are helped, they will receive reward from God. Is that because they paid for a computer? In part, yes. But mostly because they encouraged me to move from inactivity to activity—from unbelief because of my inabilities, to faith in God's ability to work through me. From being a dreamer to a realizer of dreams.

To all of you who play such a vital role in my life, I owe you. Thanks! And if you'd like, I'll even let you touch my new toy.

COFFEE AND THE CROSS

I made an important decision about 20 years ago. I decided to be a connoisseur of coffee. This was brought on while I was at a friend's house for dinner. He pulled out an electric grinder and ground his beans for a *precise* period of time. I was impressed. He then brewed what even I knew to be a fine cup of coffee.

Shortly after that meal of enlightenment, I was on a hunting trip. Following a day in the cold, we stopped by a little donut shop east of Redding for some high calorie refreshment. I was impressed by their coffee. In efforts to gain from my culinary skills, I made a long-distance phone call later that day to inquire about the kind of beans they used. With this bit of insight, I was sure to impress my friends. Imagine my embarrassment when they told me it was instant. In my view, instant coffee is only a notch or two above toxic waste. So much for any chance I might have had in getting a position at the *San Francisco Chronicle* as a restaurant critic.

Since those early days, I have put my taste buds through a series of strenuous tests, refining my abilities to recognize quality in that little bean once thought to bring healing to the body.

Several years ago we had a number of people over to our home for a meeting. An elderly woman, along with her middle-aged daughter, got excited when they heard that the coffee was ready. I saw then that I had somehow earned a reputation for brewing a better than average cup. Without them being aware, I watched as they took their first sip. As the hot Vienna Roast rolled over their tongues, they wrinkled up their faces and looked at each other as though they had found the town idiot. One turned to the other and said in a loud whisper, *"This* is the coffee we've been hearing about?" Not everyone is impressed.

Awhile back I made espresso for a couple of guests visiting our home, hoping that along with me they would enjoy one of the finer things in life. It's fun to do this for those I think might appreciate similar experiences in coffee. My guests wasted no time in letting me know what kind of garbage I was serving, saying something about using it for "road tar." Some time later we were guests in their home. When it came time for coffee, she brought me a quart of 10/40 weight automobile oil. Imagine the nerve.

My tendency toward coffee snobbery is gratifying mostly when I find people of like mind. To increase the number of those with like mind, I have been able to convert a few poor souls who through ignorance thought that coffee was that beige stuff found in the average American restaurant. I now buy coffees from South America, the Caribbean, and Africa, in a variety of roasts (all of which are dark). I even try to have decaf around for my friends who no longer can afford the buzz.

A wide assortment of coffee is fun, if the quality doesn't change. Variety in life is to be appreciated also. Learning about other peoples and cultures is helpful in reminding us of the multifaceted beauty and nature of God. We should learn to accept, with love, the uniqueness of every individual. It's a sign of maturity and godly tolerance. But this trait was never intended to cause us to entertain every spiritual flake that comes through town. Acceptance of ideas that contradict the Scriptures is similar to a local chef using just small amounts of strychnine in his cooking. "After all, we mustn't be closed to other realities." There is only one gospel. Truth is simple and complete in itself.

I have a pastoral acquaintance who recently fell into compromise through sitting under the teaching of a cult leader who started to attend his church. After being influenced by this man's charisma, he bought into his teaching. It was all in an effort to bring the reality of "inner healing" to his people. While healing of all kinds is the wonderful provision of the Lord, the devil will use the same subject to deceive those who will listen to his ideas. This became an almost unbelievable horror story with massive demonic manifestations. It has brought extensive damage to the Body of Christ in that large California community.

How did this happen to mature believers? They lost sight of the Cross. Remember, if it's not provided for in the redemptive work of Christ, you don't want it, pure and simple. The devil enthusiastically allows for the acceptance of this wonderful provision from God—healing—if we'll believe it comes through the Cross, plus something else... anything else.

The truth of the Cross is the center of all wisdom. From there the foolishness of man is clearly exposed to any who will draw near. Through death we live. By loss we gain. In humility we are exalted. And it's all because of the power of the Cross. It is the redemptive work of Christ that defines our past—forgiven; our present—accepted by God; and our future—forever reigning with Christ. The Cross dismantles all the powers of darkness, takes away the authority of sickness and disease, and destroys the sting of death and the grip of the grave. The Cross even crucified our old nature that had its claws firmly embedded in our hearts and minds. The Cross—the moment that appeared to be earth's greatest failure—was Heaven's greatest triumph.

Revel in it. Rejoice in it. But never depart from it.

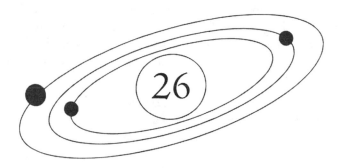

LIMITATIONS AND LIBERTIES

Several years ago I was cutting wood with a few of our diehard men. We had the job of felling a small tree (8 to 10-inch diameter) in someone's backyard, with the promise that it would become wood for our winter's heat. It was a tree that leaned toward their neighbor's fence. We had the brilliant idea of tying a rope to the tree about halfway up and then pulling it toward the owner's yard as it was being cut. Being of the brave sort, I volunteered to be the anchor at the end of the rope, kind of like in a tug-of-war. So I wrapped the rope around my waist, and solicited the support of other able-bodied men. As the tree began to fall, we pulled with all of our might. When it became evident that this was a dumb idea, all the men with options disappeared, which left me as the sole fence saver. I became a human stone in a 25-foot tall, fence-destroying slingshot. Yes, I became airborne. I don't know how far I flew, but it was my longest flight to date. Forget the rides at Disneyland; I'm a woodcutter!

Every year we try to take at least one week of our vacation in Santa Cruz with my parents. Our primary occupation during this week is either to lie or play on the beach. I work hard at doing nothing and have become quite good at it. During one such trip while my boys and I were playing Frisbee, one of them threw it hard and long. I ran about as fast as one can move in sand. Just as I was about to reach up and make another catch for the ESPN Highlight Film Archives, I ran into a 55-gallon drum, which wasn't there just a moment earlier. Someone must have put it there right after the Frisbee was thrown.

My body has been speaking to me a lot lately, saying, "We can't do that anymore" or "Perhaps you don't remember, but we never could do that!" referring to my attempt to run through solid objects.

On an earlier occasion, as a young person, I tried to run through a fence in the dark. A bunch of us were playing hide-and-seek outdoors at night. I didn't know the fence was there. As the seeker began to count, "Ten, nine, eight," I ran at the speed of light toward a stand of tress. It all happened so fast. It took me a little while to figure out why I was lying on the ground with torn pants, pain in my leg, and a flow of blood. It eventually occurred to me that I had run into something. Groping about in the dark, I soon discovered the culprit—a barbwire fence.

The apostle Paul said that a person is *"not to think of himself more highly than he ought to think, but to think soberly, as God has dealt to each one a measure of faith"* (Rom. 12:3). It actually takes faith to know what you can and can't do. "Thinking soberly" is related to faith. Faith is often considered to be a whimsical grasp at the unseen, when actually it is a levelheaded approach to life from God's point of view! While nothing is impossible with God, many things are impossible for us, except for the one who believes. Faith is the issue. Paul tells us to think according to the measure of faith given to us (see Rom. 12:3). That statement accepts that there are limits in our faith, and why not do something with what we have? If we don't, it's easy to become a careless Christian by thinking beyond our actual level of faith.

It's the wise person who knows his limitations. For example, we tend to become like the crowd with whom we spend the most time. So wisdom says to work hard at being with people who will influence you in the way you want to live. If you have a problem with alcohol, don't watch a football game with Six-pack Steve and Barroom Bill. If you intend to put the pedal to the metal, don't buy a Mustang 5.0 (unless you'll let me use it!). Wisdom has always been rather practical.

It is also wisdom to know your strengths and pour your energies into them. Many people spend a lifetime trying to correct their weaknesses, giving little time to building excellence in their strengths. Sometimes weaknesses would simply die if they didn't receive so much attention. Believe it or not, weaknesses tend to develop and not disappear when they are focused upon—even with negative attention. To pour myself into a God-given strength is to seek to honor God with His assignment for my life. It is wisdom to know both our limitations and our liberties.

I've decided to let trees fall where they may. It's their gift. And mine is to burn them.

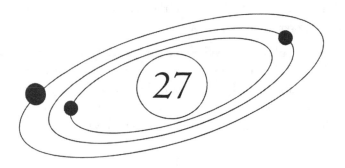

SOUNDS OF FEAR OR PEACE

I've heard it said that one of the most instinctive fears that a person has is that of noise. For this reason a baby will often cry when a door slams, or when someone raises their voice. I saw that again this past week when my classless dog, Rez, *ran over* a small child in his excitement to be alive. I'm sure that little Taylor felt overwhelmed by this huge beast knocking her featherweight body to the ground. But her tears flowed only when I firmly corrected my dog.

Rez only knows a few words. *Rez, no, sit, drop, and come*—he only knows come when it's convenient. Everything else I put into a sentence is for my benefit. For example, if I say, "Rez! You classless animal. Can't you see that there is a small child in front of you? Pay attention to me or I'll turn you into a trophy for my wall. That was a totally dumb thing to do." As I read in a cartoon once, my dog only understands, "Rez! *%#@+_*&%@!#%^x%^$ $#!%$ ^ **(). !>)*^$#."

When I was a teenager, I worked for a man who built and installed garage doors. One day while we were installing a large door in a shop that was built for big trucks, something happened that caused my heart to leap, almost becoming airborne. Apparently, a valve on an air compressor broke loose, creating a sound similar to a 747 landing in that little building. What made it worse was that no one expected it. I wish I had a video of that 5-second period of panic. There was no place to run, but we did. I quickly took about a thousand misdirected stutter steps and grabbed a ladder to hide behind. It was the closest thing next to me. I know that made no sense, but fear seldom does.

Several years ago while deer hunting, I was walking on the top of a ridge. Out of nowhere a military jet skimmed the treetops above my head. In one moment it was just me surrounded by the music of the forest—a wonderful mixture of birds, squirrels, and silence—and the next, that 747 from the earlier year came back to get whatever years I might have had leftover from our previous encounter.

One Halloween (it's hard to understand how I could have given any honor to that unholy day!), again during my high school years, I went into a haunted house that was created by some friends. As I walked cautiously through the hallway, someone jumped out and screamed. And I nearly jumped out of my skin. In that millisecond of fright someone with a Polaroid took a picture. It was quite humorous. It was of me holding onto the guy in front of me for dear life.

Those kinds of fears come from sudden and/or loud noises. Rock music is proof that one can acquire a taste for something that once instinctively caused fear. Even though I have the acquired taste, I draw the line short of noise for noise's sake. But, I guess even that is a matter of opinion.

About the coolest guy I knew liked the sound of static on his radio. All that annoying crackle and popping was appealing to him. Come to think of it, he probably knew some cool guy that liked it and acquired a taste for it in order to be cool as well. Following our deep conversation on the subject, I, too, wanted to like static. So I would turn on my radio, put the dial between stations, and try to enjoy the noise. It was to be my ticket to coolness. I never got there though. It got on my nerves. It was an acquired taste that I couldn't acquire.

In contrast to the noise that brings fear, there are the sounds of peace and joy. I worked on a survey crew in the mountains of southern Trinity County right out of high school. One day, while working in the woods, we heard the most beautiful sound. It was hard to distinguish the nature of this sound, but it was definitely music. Beautiful music. Throughout that morning we heard the musical notes build in intensity and subside. They would come and go. Awhile later we discovered the source of the music; it came from the resident of the "woods." He had been playing his tenor saxophone. It was hard to figure out the kind of instrument being played because of the echo through the mountains. Nature's reverb. It was wonderful…and oh, so peaceful.

My dad borrowed a houseboat so he could take my brother and me to Shasta Lake for a couple of days of fishing. Prior to that I had bought a flute. At night I went out to the roof of the houseboat with my little instrument. While I never became very good, I could play a bit. I wanted someone else to hear the music of one instrument echoing through the mountainous region of Shasta Lake. Sound travels so well on water that it seemed to be the perfect place to play to an unsuspecting crowd of campers.

There are sounds of peace, and there are sounds of fear. A wonderful truth for believers is that any sound that brings peace to you will bring fear to the powers of darkness. If it encourages you, it will discourage the devil. If it gives you joy, it will cause the devil sorrow. And all the while you are encouraged, God is honored. He takes delight in the sounds that refresh His people.

> *Blessed are the people who know the joyful sound! They shall walk, O Lord, in the light of Your countenance* (Psalm 89:15).

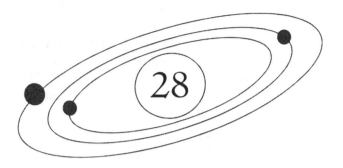

TRUE HAPPINESS

I recently stood in line at an Albertson's grocery store. In front of me was a young man who looked quite old. He was buying a bottle of vodka. His clothes were covered with about as much dirt and grease as could possibly stick to fabric, giving away his probably homeless condition. He spoke to the cashier of a job that was out there somewhere with his name on it. That job, he felt, would make him happy. But, I guess, the bottle would do for now.

I was in the Santa Rosa area for a week of ministry. Their economy seems to be booming. New buildings are going up all over this former farming community. The new car lots are filled with people who would be happy if they could just have the newest, the latest. . . .

The churches in that area are just like the churches most anywhere—many successes, many failures. In moments of transparency it seems that the hurts and needs of the people outweigh the apparent growth. Most of today's growth is transfer growth anyway. Most of us pastors would like to believe that what we have is the hottest thing going, so therefore transfer growth (people coming to our church from one down the road) is people coming home to where they should have been in the first place. But deep in our hearts, we know differently. We have strong points. We have weak points. And what people are looking for from us will determine whether or not we will be successful in meeting their needs. Many such pastors would be happy if only their sheep were happy.

About 20 miles to the south is a classy shopping center. Some of California's finer stores are in this mall. I watched as people shopped for joy. But what they were really shopping for was not for sale.

I have never had the wealth that these people seem to have. But I do have the kind of wealth where I had money leftover after the bills to spend on whatever my heart desired (up to a few hundred dollars). And I guess whether that happens to a person once or a thousand times, they would then qualify as wealthy. In those times of being able to fulfill my own desires, I usually found it to be overrated and disappointing. The only time a material thing has brought real happiness was when that item was used for a higher purpose than the purpose of simply owning something.

The class that I came to teach was about to start, and I had just found a quaint little coffee roasting store. I ran in quickly to get my cup of Americano coffee (half dark roast coffee and half espresso) to take to class. I had purposed to stop by later for a longer lasting moment of pleasure, probably with a newspaper. When I returned, I ordered a double espresso. My family will tell you that I look forward to these moments, when there are no other demands but to sit quietly, perhaps reading something simple (if I have to read something challenging it ruins the moment), and drinking a pleasant cup of coffee (known as high octane, nuclear waste to some of my friends). I was happy.

I was teaching at a Bible school. One of the young ladies had just been served divorce papers and was devastated. She was crying out to God to restore her marriage. That would make her happy.

The teaching time went well. There was also a strong prophetic anointing for personal ministry. That is always fun—true pleasure.

Alone in a motel room, I began to think of the things that make me happy. Here are a few things that came to mind.

Quiet time, with a clean conscience.

Time with friends—the kind of friends who make you glad you are you and happy to be with them.

Ideas that hold a promise and a hope to them.

Being out in the woods, seeing life go on without me.

Writing...sometimes. Finishing a writing project...always.

Fishing—when I actually understand what's going on in the water around me and present the fly properly. It's the rare moment when knowledge and skill meet, and are then rewarded.

Reading things that encourage and challenge.

Premium coffee—dark and bitter—with something sweet. (My mother once walked in on my grandmother as she was eating a spoonful of sugar in the middle of the night. Grandma, then 80-something, responded with, "When you get older, your body requires more sweets." My sentiments exactly!)

Something sweet—European chocolate.

Lifting weights.

Being with my family.

Seeing people happy.

Eating a good meal.

Writing such a list seems a little vain. Still, there is one item that so supersedes all the others that they are meaningless without this one component—God's favor.

There is a moment coming that will be the most important moment of our lives. It is that break in time when the Father will declare to those who are His, *"Well done, good and faithful servant…Enter into the joy of your Master"* (see Matt. 25:21). That is His *amen* to our obedience. Any suffering or loss, any sacrifice or season of endurance, will all be engulfed by an eternity without tears or sorrow, and an overwhelming joy that only grows and never diminishes.

I am convinced that all the things that make life enjoyable are little tastes of Heaven. But without receiving God's favor through the offering of His Son Jesus, Heaven will only be something tasted, locked up in time. But for those who have found their delight, not in things, not in this world, but in knowing Him, every little moment of pleasure just makes us hungrier for Heaven.

So what is the cost of happiness? It's costly, but it's paid for—by the Ultimate Merchant. Relax, work faithfully, and enjoy with thankfulness.

SING A NEW SONG

It was a very special evening in the fall of 1968. My FM radio was next to my bed and ready to take me on a journey. I had looked forward to this moment ever since I had heard that The Beatles' new *White Album* was to be debuted that night. The station that I listened to was the only one I had ever heard of that played Beatles music exclusively. This occasion was even more unique in that they were going to play the entire two-album set over the air in one setting.

The sounds that I heard that evening were new. Never before had I heard a musical group play such variety, all of which I thought was excellent and creative. Oh, the pleasure of new music!

A couple of years later I had a similar experience when I picked up the newly released Janis Joplin album at the local Licorice Pizza Record Store. It was released right after her overdose-induced death. I brought it to the home of a family I was staying with at the time. For the next several days I sat mesmerized at what I considered to be an incredible new piece of music. Her gut-wrenching vocals and *bluesy* band excited me. I wanted to do very little but listen, and then listen some more. What a gift she had. She sang with raw emotion. I was so glad for her music.

The Beatles broke up, and Paul did his own album. He was always my favorite, so it was natural for me to save to buy his new recording as soon as it became available. I did. Wow! It was like Christmas to receive such a gift.

The first time you hear a piece of music is like a voyage into uncharted waters. Surprises await you around every corner. And when the talent is exceptional, there are few surprises that bring anything but sheer pleasure.

Times have changed. It's no longer albums or four-tracks. It's metal tape and CDs. And even those mediums are facing technological evolution. I too have changed. While I still appreciate the musical talents of the McCartney's of this world, their view of life is so drastically different from mine that I have chosen not to volunteer to be taught empty philosophies in their classrooms. It's a personal decision. But I still love good music.

The experiences that I mentioned are few and far between, be it from Christian or non-Christian artists. Every new piece of music from Michael Omartian, or the now disbanded 2nd Chapter of Acts or the forever-young Rez Band has been an enjoyable experience. But the one occasion that stands out in my mind as a totally new adventure took place one afternoon in 1977. Bob Kilpatrick and I went to my home to listen to several new albums that had just come to the bookstore that I managed for the church. One of those recordings was from a personal favorite, Phil Keaggy. We listened to his album first. When it was over I put on one from another artist. We could only handle a few cuts and would then go back to Phil. The other pieces of music would have been good on any other day. But, because I first listened to them on *that* day, I could hardly ever listen to them again.

Phil is a mega talent, the standard by which other guitarists are measured. But this album was more than a fine display of talent. This one had a new sound. It's so rare to have a recording provide the canvas for artistic ability *and* something fresh. This one did both.

Bob and I had discovered something rich that day: a new piece of music. Every song was a treasure. We had laid claim to a mine filled with gold.

Have you ever wondered how God views our music? We know that music exists in Heaven and that God sings. But how does He respond to our music?

God is the One who gives music as a gift. He is also the One who gives musical abilities to individuals. Whether that person is Jimmy Hendrix or Phil Keaggy, their talent came from God. What each person does with what they've been given is up to them. Phil Collins is not talented because of the devil's inspiration. It's because he was made in the image of God, and God gives each person special abilities. And I respect the person and his or her gift.

I have a feeling that part of the National Treasure of the Kingdom of God is the music that we give to Him. I also think that when we sing a new song to the Lord (one that is spontaneous and from the heart), we give something that would be for Him the equivalent of the experiences that I mentioned from my own life. Is it possible that God could receive our love expressions in a new song with the same sense of expectancy that we might have listening to a new recording? I think so—probably even more so.

Sing to the Lord a new song! It's a good idea to do this daily. The words don't have to rhyme. The melody doesn't have to stir the hearts of politicians to pursue world peace, nor the brushes of great artists to paint a masterpiece. The song just needs to be real and from the heart. If it is, God is moved.

Go ahead, sing a new song to God. I think I just heard Him say, "Make My day!"

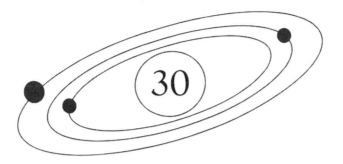

SAFE IN THE CENTER

Which is the safer place to be—in the fiery furnace with Shadrach and the boys, or with the rest of the Jews who bowed before a false god and were under the protection of King Nebuchadnezzar? Which is the more comfortable place to be—in the middle of a war by God's design or walking on the rooftop of a palace (like David) looking at a beautiful woman who would forever mark your life with failure?

Where would you rather be—en route to India and back during threatened terrorist activities or seemingly safe at home, knowing that it was God who opened the door to go? The center of God's will is the safest place to be. And if we die, we couldn't have asked for better circumstances to die under.

Some wonder if it is wise for me to go to India where there is all this "war" in the air. I am not wise enough to see tomorrow. Only Jesus sees all the details of all my days. My wisdom is being stretched just to recognize an "open door" for ministry. Until He closes a door of opportunity, I must continue doing what He last told me to do. Actually, I'm hoping that all this international conflict will make this trip better. Why? Because I expect more people to pray. Thanks, and please do.

Come to think of it, maybe I am safer on an international flight than here at home. After all, I have traveled around the world telling people that the center of the universe is Weaverville, California!

I love you so much and give thanks to God for all of you.

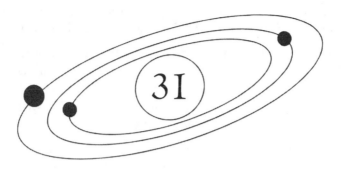

FINDING YOUR NICHE

Years ago there was a humorous story going around about what would happen if you played country music backward. Of course, this was a takeoff from what many have done with Rock 'n' Roll, looking for secret messages that would subtly communicate cultish messages to the listener. The joke went on to say that if country music was played backward, you'd get your job back, your wife would return, and even your dog would come home. This past week my dog came home, and I don't listen to country music in either direction.

Rez, for those of you unfamiliar with my ongoing saga, is a German Shorthair. He has had an unusual impact on my family, mostly from what he has eaten or destroyed. He's back from the trainer and is ready to hunt. He's even more civilized, which could mean little, considering *from whence he came.*

It looks like the one that almost ate me out of house and home may be a greater blessing than I expected. His hyperactivity has been *diagnosed* as a passion to hunt. When he is in the right environment, his gift shines. What once drove us nuts is now his most valued trait. In fact, the trainer painted an interesting picture for me. He can break Rez of his overzealous approach to life. But in doing so, it would break him of his unique hunting instincts that are good for field trials—a hunting test for both dog and hunter that proves the quality of the dog. Or, he could train him in a way to get the maximum out of his gift and multiply our opportunity for breeding (with the customary stud fee—about $400 a time).

The attribute that almost got him mounted by a local taxidermist is now being preserved at all costs. It could supply us with the finances needed to pay for the damages he has done to our home and personal property. Of course that would be *many* female Shorthairs from now…but it could happen. Through this whole ordeal I always believed (or at least hoped) that he would be a good dog. We just had to confirm that this was his *gift*.

This reminds me of my friend, Larry. We both played football at Ambassador High School in Downey, California. I was never big, but Larry was even smaller. He had good instincts for the game but never stood out as a player, mostly because of his size. One day our coach decided to put him in a game as a defensive halfback. An average player became a star defensive player. Larry found his niche and grew in excellence.

I heard an interview last night with one of the 49ers' assistant coaches regarding their victory over the Dallas Cowboys this past week (a victory I'm still savoring—mmmm good!). Following his interview, the radio announcer mentioned how many teams this coach had worked for with little success. It seemed that his talent plus the 49ers game plan and personality made for a perfect marriage. He has found his place and is flourishing.

Studies have been done in corporations of America to examine where employees have their greatest fulfillment. A problem they have discovered is that people who have proven themselves in their positions are often promoted beyond their capabilities. One who is an excellent salesman may not be a good manager of salesmen. Yet it is often true that the great salesman is promoted to the position of manager and ceases to enjoy and flourish in his work. It takes wisdom to know what we're good at and contentment to stay there. Unhappiness should never be the fruit of success. Perhaps that's one reason God says that when he gives wealth, He *adds no sorrow to it* (see Prov. 10:22).

Everyone has a place where God has assigned him or her to excel. No one is left out of this picture. One great tragedy is that there are many who live an entire lifetime never feeling as though they accomplished what they were born to accomplish. We need to achieve. It is a God-given drive.

It is sometimes thought that the drive to produce in life is always a personal crusade for selfish ambition. Not true. It is God who has given us abilities and talents. It is He who has given us imagination and creativity. And it has been God who has given us the command to contribute to society through our labors. It's nice to know that we can also *enjoy* this assignment.

Achieve! With one word of caution. Culture, good or bad, should not define our assignment in life. We are people of another Kingdom, with completely different values. Only the King is worthy of defining our place in life. And He does so lovingly, with wisdom, purpose, and hope, all with our well-being in mind. *Just do it!* For Him. Remember, He adds no sorrow.

Who says that time doesn't heal all wounds? Would you believe that my wife is as happy to have Rez home as I am? In fact, she, being the one who insisted that I build a kennel outside for him because *he will not be in the house when you're not home*, has even allowed Rez to sleep in our bedroom at night because it's cold and wet outside. And when I'm not home...Rez is indoors enjoying her company. Actually, this was made possible because somewhere in his time away he learned a little class. And now it's my duty to give him the opportunity to do what he was born to do.

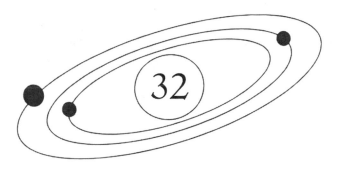

FERVENT PRAYER

"The effective [fervent] *prayer of a righteous man can accomplish much"* (James 5:16 NASB). Motivation is something that without, we accomplish nothing. With it, we have a sense of conviction and direction. Herein lies the battle of the drive to excel versus apathetic contentment.

This area is one that we are responsible to maintain and energize. My personal drive in prayer is fueled by hearing the testimony of the Lord, the promises of His Word, and by His stirrings in my heart as I spend time with Him. Fervent prayer is motivated prayer. And with it answers are apprehended.

There are two balancing qualities to "red hot" prayer. The first is that we are to sense God's *burden*. This is where we come to know His grief. It is shared with us only partially, that we might become partners with Him as He intercedes for the situation in question. Someone has said that Christians who go nowhere are tearless Christians. Second, fervent prayer has direction, or in other words, *vision*. Power that is not channeled is dangerous. Vision is what gives our prayer a "track" to run on. Without vision, a burden is a hopeless pain. With the element of hope, a wayward circumstance is brought into the realm of God's promises.

These two qualities give us the protective boundaries for effective prayer. Because we don't know how to pray as we should, we must ask the Holy Spirit to teach us. Part of His assignment on this earth is to pray through us. He is the source for both the burden and the vision. Because of this, it should be no surprise that this kind of prayer "accomplishes much."

DISCOVERIES IN PRAYER

I had hoped that by giving myself to more prayer, it would become a time of great spiritual discovery. It has been, but in a much different way than I had expected.

I thought that I would discover a source of real power through prayer. Instead I found weakness—mine. It seemed that with more prayer I would rise to a place of powerful ministry. Instead, I am filled with an awareness of inability to handle power. My eyes have turned from my grand future to a grace-filled present. I'm not disappointed, just surprised.

I figured that with more prayer I would become pure and holy. It seems that instead, I have become aware of my impurity. When I thought that my heart would jump at the chance to be holy, I found it to be coarse and vain. I do sense a change happening in me, but I realize now that it's not as much from my heart as it is from His. I'm not disappointed, just surprised.

More prayer appeared to be the key to the miraculous. Certainly if I pray more there will be more miracles happening through my life. It's true that I see more miracles. But so far it's not that they have increased as much as I see my world differently. I'm not disappointed, just surprised.

With more prayer, I would discover the "riches of Christ," right? My first discovery was my spiritual poverty. As for His riches, they fill my heart only as I see my need. I'm not disappointed, just surprised.

If there was one thing that I knew for sure, it was that more prayer brought more answers. My shock came when I realized that I don't have *more* as much as I have *different* answers. I'm not disappointed, just surprised.

I invite you to a life of more prayer. But you need to know, it's probably not what you think. Is it the way to fulfilled dreams and desires? Yes and no. I didn't get what I wanted. But what I've got is what I want.

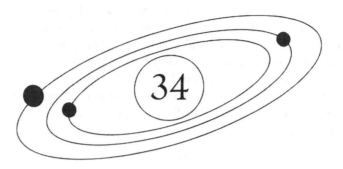

PRECIOUS

My wife and kids have been in Mexico this past week on the Mountain Chapel outreach. It has been my responsibility to care for my daughter's dog, Precious. Every day she looks forward to Beni and Leah coming home. When I open the front door, she runs to the car and looks, sometimes at each door, for the women of our household to get out. I am second choice at best. Now I don't want to imply that this dog doesn't like me. It's that she only likes me indoors. She will jump into my lap, sleep next to me on the couch, and many other things that would make you think that this dog thinks I'm special. But when we step outside, something happens. It's like her true feelings for me come out, indicating that what she does in the house is really a lie. The great outdoors becomes her great escape.

When I come home she barks and runs through the house, jumping for joy, because this wonderful person has come home to play with her. I do all that you're supposed to do—scratch her, wrestle with her, and even talk funny (like all dog owners do when they speak affectionately to their pets). Then we step outside. She takes one look at me and attempts to get raptured. She actually jumped into a neighbor's car, with them in it, in an attempt to get away from me. The previous day she tried to get into a neighbor's house. (I remind you, these are all people that we've never met—we're staying at the Miller's house.) Again, Precious was trying to get away from me. I'm telling you, this dog has it in for me.

It's the strangest thing, but I think I've seen this before—in the church of all places. There are some (none of *us!*) who gather on Sunday morning with the greatest of excitement, glad to be able to share with other believers the joy of worshiping God (indoors, of course). But as soon as the service is over—gone!

The mystery of the great outdoors again casts its spell as believers jump into any car going somewhere else. The invaluable gift of fellowship is again laid aside in favor of isolation and all the other wonderful alternatives. These people can be soooo warm on Sunday morning, only to run at the thought of getting to really know someone. Of course, that's not us. But we all know this kind of Christian, don't we? I've never seen it firsthand, but I've heard about it. Or maybe I read about it in the *Pastor's Anonymous Recovery Manual*, under the heading of "How We Survived the Dreaded 'Dog's Disease.'" At any rate, I knew that I had seen the antics of our dog Precious before.

I may have to live with a dog that thinks I'm dirt (outside), but I don't have to tolerate the great escape in my personal life. Fellowship is best at room temperature, in the sacrifice dimension. Give and enjoy.

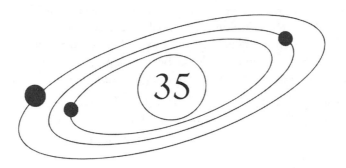

Exposure Creates Interest

My wife laughs at me. She considers it funny the way I approach new interests. It seems perfectly logical to me.

In 1973 I became interested in fly-fishing. An old-timer promised to teach me how to cast, and did. Another friend, a postal worker, gave me an undeliverable magazine that was all about fly-fishing. That's when the snowball began to roll. I subscribed to that magazine, and then another, and now...I'll leave that for Beni to describe.

I soon joined a book club focused only on outdoor sports. I was able to purchase many fine books on the subject. My knowledge has been increasing in proportion to the stack of literature in my room. Today I have many books, rods, reels, and well over a decade of magazine subscriptions (all in order, according to date). If I seem to lose interest, I pick up a magazine and the fever hits. And can you believe it, Beni laughs at me for that?

Anything that I want to do, whether it be a hobby or an activity, I try to do it well. In order to be able to do a good job, I read and learn from others who already know more than me. When I started weight training seven months ago, I began buying magazines on the subject, as well as having those "in the know" help me so that I could do it intelligently. This body of mine, that was built on Häagen-Dazs and chocolate truffles, has gone into shock in recent months. I'm learning about nutrition. In doing so, I'm more confident in my workout. If I get lax, I read, and presto—the hunger to work out comes again.

What I have described is a natural law. Exposure to something, in a favorable setting, creates interest. The effect of this law is multiplied in spiritual things. If you are weak in prayer, read on prayer. Books of great men and women of God can be very inspirational and instructional. But more than that, study the subject in your Bible. The reason that this principle is much more powerful in the spiritual is because of the power of God's Word to renew. If I have been strong in prayer, and today I'm not, the Word cuts and exposes the motive of the heart. In other words, the Bible not only tells me what to do, it exposes what caused the decline, and at the same time it gives me the hunger for what is right.

We *must* bring renewal to ourselves. In part this is done by our approach to the Word when we're in need. What may be strange in my hobbies is the way of *life* in spiritual matters. Immerse yourself in His Word. I dare you. You'll never be the same.

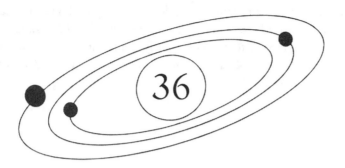

HEARING GOD

This past week a friend told me of his difficulty in hearing the "still, small voice" of the Lord. But then he said that he had no problem hearing the "big, loud voice" of his wife. I laughed and promised to quote him. His comment was not an indictment against his wife, but was instead a confession of his need to hear from God better. She was willing to say what she felt needed to be said. And it was neither still nor small.

Hearing the voice of God is probably the most sought after skill of the believer. It means the difference between success and failure in many cases. Jesus was the best example of this, as He shows us that His whole ministry depended on knowing what the Father was saying and doing. And so we spend our lives learning to recognize His voice.

There are two things that help us maximize our efforts in learning this skill:

1. The Scriptures help us know the mind of God. His revealed will helps us to be able to judge that thought or impression to see whether or not it is biblical. Getting to know our Bibles is a lifelong joy.

2. Listening to godly people can help us as well. Sometimes it might best be referred to as that "big, loud voice" of the people of God. Certainly, not everything that is said by a believer is correct, as none of us is infallible, but devotion to the people of God will help us with our hearing.

Remember, we are all just learning. And the key to learning in the Kingdom of God is willingness, not sweat!

My son, Eric, has a significant hearing loss. The responsibility to be heard is mine. I make all the necessary adjustments—speaking louder if needed, making sure that he is looking at me, etc.—in order to be heard. Our heavenly Father is the same way. He takes the responsibility to be heard. Being hard of hearing is not a sin. Hardness of heart is. So don't sweat it. Be willing.

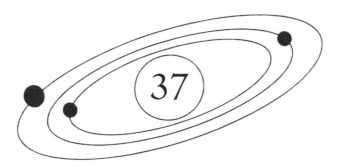

IMAGINATION

"It was an unusually dark December afternoon. The clouds had blocked what little sun was available that far into winter. The old house was cold. Electric wall heaters were no match for the arctic breezes that blew on that particular day. Even though the windows were closed, the sheer curtains moved as I had hoped they would that previous summer. The high ceiling seemed to hold captive all the available heat. And the hardwood floors were all too willing to give it away."

God gave each of us an imagination with which to enjoy ideas. Can you feel the chill I described? Have you been in a similar house? It's God's gift of sight!

The greatest authors have a way of capturing our attention while releasing our imagination. C.S. Lewis was a master at this. And he could do it for children or adults, all in the same sentence. Another such author is a man named Capstick. I am reading about his years of being a professional hunter in Africa. Few people that I have ever read can describe a situation as he can, although I'm glad I didn't read it before my trip to Africa this past August. He provoked a new "awe" in me for this faraway continent.

It disturbs me to see Christians become mechanical and lose imagination. While some have thought it to be unspiritual, it is God's way of letting us see ideas. If satan can rob us of imagination, he takes away our creative edge and spoils within us the heart of the child. With it we can see our greatest achievements before they happen, or we can devise the most hideous crimes known to man. How well does your imagination work? Is it active when you read the Bible, pray, or hear a testimony?

Your imagination is the canvas that the Greatest Author and Artist—Holy Spirit—would like to use in painting His creative ideas into your life. Keep it active. Keep it clean. And He'll keep it worthwhile.

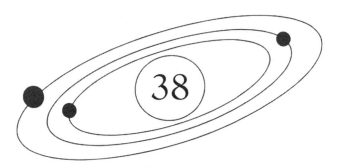

QUIET TIME

Yesterday I spent about four and a half hours with other Assembly of God pastors from Northern California. We met to pray. Nothing spectacular happened—unless you count the presence of a Holy God through the blood of Jesus. We took time to be still before God. I discovered again that when you don't do this kind of prayer often, you have many more things to repent of—careless attitudes, secret sins of envy, pride, and the like. Maybe that's why it's so hard to take the time.

It is said that the lack of solitude is at the heart of some of our country's greatest ills. Being alone with God is more than a duty to pray through a list of needs and desires. It's a reminder of priorities. Quiet time forces busyness to find its victims elsewhere.

I recently read a story about a young man who was a new employee at a big corporation. He noticed that a fellow worker spent a lot of time staring out the window, seemingly getting little work done. Being concerned, he went to his superior. The boss answered his complaint with something like, "Leave him alone. Last month, looking out that window, he had an idea that saved us a million dollars."

It's ironic that many of us have reasoned that we are to work hard and long to be more productive, when in God's Kingdom, less is often more. We have more financially after the tithe and offering has been given. There is more to our week when we honor God with a day of rest. And our days are more productive when we put God first and sit quietly at His feet. Yes, less is more with God.

Television reveals America's appetite. From violence to materialism, we hunger for things that have grown out of the soil void of quiet time. "America, be still and know that Jesus is God." Is it that simple? I think so.

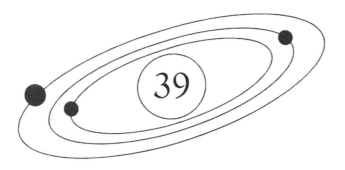

PROVERBS

The gospel is able to touch every culture, regardless of that culture's weaknesses. One of our great stumbling blocks is the "Western rational mind." We tend to reduce spiritual truths to formulas and guarantees, similar to what you get with a new washer and dryer. Truth is spiritual, and can only be fully apprehended by the spirit within us. Yet in spite of our rational downfall, God has a book in the Bible especially for us. Proverbs. Why? In it God says, "If you do this, I will do that." It's very cut and dried, almost as though God ordained the concept of formulas just for us.

For example, we know that the fear of the Lord is the beginning of wisdom (see Ps. 111:10). But the question is asked, "How do I get the fear of the Lord?" Proverbs 2:1-5 (NASB) gives us the answer: *"If you will receive My words, and treasure My commandments within you…if you cry for discernment, lift your voice for understanding; if you seek her as silver, and search for her as for hidden treasures, then you will discern the fear of the Lord…."* "If" we receive, treasure, cry for, seek, and search for, "then" you will discover. Simple, but profound!

Has God compromised His own gospel by giving us formulas? Of course not. He has invited us to reason with Him. He is not intimidated by our culture or our ways. Instead, He comes to us in the Proverbs to challenge us to discover Him through obedience. For example: If I obey His Word regarding giving, He will provide for me. But the greater benefit is that if I wish, I can get to know the Provider. And it all began because I received His challenge and obeyed.

In the rocky days ahead, it will become more and more apparent who has founded their lives on this gift from God, the Bible. Read it, memorize it, and live by it.

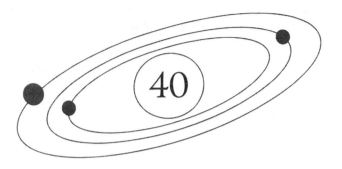

LESSONS IN PRAYER

I was troubled one night this past week as I went to bed—worried is a more honest word. The power of anxiety is similar to the power of faith, except it works in the opposite direction. One gives life and the other gives death.

The logical thing to do in that situation is to pray, and so I did. Yet nothing seemed to happen. My heart was still anxious, and the much needed night of sleep seemed more and more unlikely. Trusting God brings us into a place of rest, which I need desperately.

I got up and knelt at my bedside (kneeling is not a required posture for prayer—it was simply my choice for the sake of humility and discipline). My prayers "broke through" when I stirred up my own heart of faith to consider God and His promises. In that situation, passive prayer is no more than a worry or complaint session with God. I've had many of them. And while those prayers temporarily ease the conscience concerning our need to pray, they do little to affect eternity. On the other hand, aggressive prayer is faith-powered, and it enables us to tap into God's solutions for our needs. The mistake that many make is to think that we must be emotionally strong to pray aggressively. Wrong! That lie is to intimidate us from reaching out for an answer in our greatest time of need.

Rest came quickly to my heart, and a good night's sleep soon followed. I have hope in God for what troubled me. And even more important to me is this: I have a fresh understanding of what it is to trust God.

In our Western culture, learning is evident by the student being able to recite certain facts or express certain ideas. We are concept oriented. On the other hand, to the Eastern mind (which is the biblical culture) learning is proven by experience. If you're anything like me, you get frustrated when what you've learned doesn't work—meaning that the latest formula I memorized didn't produce the right results. The sobering lesson is this: we've not learned until we've taken truth and applied it successfully. Only then can we say we've learned.

This lesson on prayer, simple as it may be, is worth more to me than a stack of books on the subject. And it only took moments of time and the willingness to "provoke" myself out of the place of lethargy into the place of aggressive faith—out of complaint into the promise.

"As God has dealt to each one a measure of faith" (Rom. 12:3). The size is unimportant. Faith grows with use. Also, it is never evident when we try to measure it. It is only seen by its fruit—which means I must use it by seeking God concerning what matters to me. Using what we have been given is our mission in life. One day I will stand before Him, and I'll be required to return to Him the fruit of what was given to me—*"to whom much is given... much will be required"* (Luke 12:48). Oh what a day!

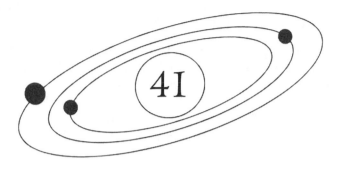

WATCHING YOUR HEART

Solomon said that hunger is what motivates a man to work harder. Elsewhere in Proverbs it says that men have been known to steal because of this desire. Whether it is the hunger for food or for reaching a personal goal, it is the one thing that influences our thoughts, ambitions, and values. Everything from the great accomplishments of science to the most brutal crimes comes about because of a hunger expressed in life. A major question to be asked is, "Can we control what we hunger for?" The biblical answer to that would be, without question, "Yes, we can, and we must control it." If it were impossible to control appetites, we would have to say that we serve a cruel God. He commands us to hunger for Him. Since we know God has provided a way for it to be done, how do we do it?

James says that if a man can control his mouth, he can control anything. Jesus said that what comes out of our mouths really comes from our heart (see Matt. 12:34). The heart is the seat of moral and spiritual values. The beginning place in the control of our pursuits in life is the ministry to our own hearts. With this in mind, let's consider our first responsibility. *"Watch over your heart with all diligence…"* (Prov. 4:23 NASB). Our hearts are similar to a beautiful garden. It may be a prize-winner today, but in not too long a period of time it can become a disaster without some practical maintenance. We have been called to be a "watchman of the heart."

I keep watch over two things continually.

1. Does my hunger for God affect my desire in life, or is it visa versa? One of the Wesley brothers said, "Whatever cools my affections for Christ, that is the world." In the natural we are concerned when our children show a loss of appetite for any length of time. So it is in

the spiritual. Lack of hunger spells sickness and disorder and must be attended to immediately.

2. In a practical sense, what are my desires in life? These are the things that make up my dreams and ambitions. Are they Christ-centered or do I receive the glory? How important are these dreams? Can I receive adjustments in my desires in order to fit God's plan, or does my will matter the most? These questions should be asked more frequently in one form or another by anyone seeking to know God more fully and desiring to stay in the mainstream of His will. Our thoughts and reactions to difficult situations can be indicators of our life's desires.

With this in mind, how can we keep our hearts in continual maintenance? How can I redirect any straying desires? These are the questions I will try to answer next.

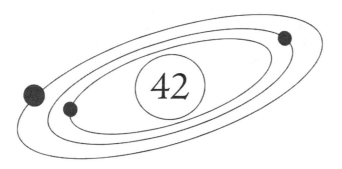

KEYS TO HUNGER

We discussed our hunger for God and how it affects our entire Christian life. Now we look at "how to redirect straying desires."

The beginning place for dealing with the heart is honesty. We must recognize sin and/or disorder and call it for what it is. This is the act of confession. It must take place before the Lord, and at times it should be shared with another brother or sister in the Lord. They in turn can help us to be honest and to walk out our commitment by providing a "checks and balances" system through a close relationship.

From honesty and confession, we go to the four main sources that God has given to us to keep us hungry for Him.

1. The Word of God. The Word exposes ill-directed desire or motives. It also creates hunger in anyone who approaches it in humility, with a willingness to obey.

2. God's presence. His anointing leads us into that which is true and stable. We can trust Him. As long as we value being in God's presence, we can be assured that we will not lack in our love for Him. Isaiah the prophet said, *"How blessed are all those who long for Him"* (Isa. 30:18 NASB).

3. Fellowship with people committed to walking with Jesus is an inspiration and should be utilized by each of us. They, in a sense, are salt on our tongues, making us thirsty for God.

4. Ministry. Being exposed to the needs greater than experience does a wonderful work in creating hunger. Hunger is really only the result of seeing our need. One sure way to see our own need is to serve people.

As some may have noticed, we used these areas in describing the four corner posts for maturity a couple of years ago. Whether we call them the "posts of maturity" or "sources to maintain hunger for God" is not important. What is important is that this is part of God's economy to keep us fit. Make use of them and we overcome. Ignore them and we are overcome.

Let us say together with King David, *"One thing I have asked from the Lord, that shall I seek; that I may dwell in the house of the Lord all the days of my life, to behold the beauty of the Lord and meditate in His temple"* (Ps. 27:4 NASB).

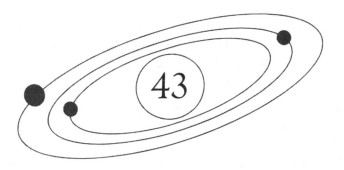

A FISH STORY

Fly-fishing is a "gentleman's sport." I enjoy it anyway. As mentioned previously, a saintly man taught me how to cast a fly in 1973. We enjoyed God and His creation together, and I have great memories of those times.

Early in my fly-fishing career I saw a cartoon that seemed to speak volumes about this great sport. A couple of bait fishermen were walking back to the car from a day of fishing. They were very unkempt, filthy, poorly dressed, a can of worms and other hardware hanging out of their pockets, rods and tackle boxes in one hand, and a whole mess of large fish in the other. They had grumpy expressions on their faces. Next to these joyless men walked a fly fisherman with a spring in his step. He was neatly dressed, carrying expensive fishing gear, with an expression of joy on his face and one 8-inch trout in his hand.

It's all a matter of perspective.

I've taught a number of people how to cast a fly. In fact, one guy I taught to fly-fish spent so much money at the local fly shop that the owner thanked me. He pointed to one section of his new building, saying, "What Larry spent in here enabled me to pay for this part of the building." I think he was kidding.

A common place to take my students is Lewiston Lake. When you're in a boat in the middle of a lake it's hard to get your line tangled in bushes and trees. One such student was named Dave. As we worked on his casting, I noticed a fish rising next to some bushes about 75 yards away (fish come to the surface of the water and "sip" freshly hatched insects; we call this "rising"). After practicing for a reasonable amount of time, it seemed to be the opportunity to get him into a fish.

We approached carefully, as fish of this sort spook easily. Dave made several casts to the unsuspecting trout. The challenge was much too soon. Afraid that he'd put the trout down (scare him out of being hungry), I took my rod in hand and put the fly on the trout's dinner plate. And according to the script that every fisherman would write for himself, Mr. Trout took it with gusto.

After landing the fish, we went back to the middle of the lake to practice his cast some more. It was improving to the point that I thought he might be able to present his fly without frightening every fish in our part of the lake. Again I notice a feeding fish. We approached with caution. Unfortunately, he couldn't quite deliver his imitation in an appealing way. I picked up my rod again, wanting to teach him by example. And again the story couldn't have been more to my favor had it been written by my own mother. The fish took my presentation with conviction. I later heard that Dave went home and told his wife, "Bill catches fish at will!"

It wasn't too long after our initial expedition that Dave and I fished other waters. From belly boats (inner tubes set up for fishing...some with three bedrooms, two bathrooms, and a double car garage) he had about a zillion rises to his fly. I had a few. He caught four fish. I caught less. When he pointed out that the student had out-fished the teacher, I made up a new rule: "It's not how many fish you catch, it's the percentage of fish that rise to your fly that you actually hook." It was the only way I could win. Although he appeared puzzled, he agreed, probably out of respect for the teacher. A student should never out-fish the teacher, at least not until he has been fishing for many years. On our next outing he beat me in both categories, the amount of fish and the new rule, percentage. I didn't want to make up any more new rules. He might still be out-fishing me today had I not admitted, "The student beat the teacher."

Pride is said to be the root of all sin. And considering how big sin is, this root system must be massive!

Much like the devil, pride doesn't always come to us wearing a red rubber suit. Anyone can spot the ugly trait in the person who seeks power, glory, and attention. But did you know that it has a quiet twin called *false humility?* It rises to power in the ones who work to put themselves down. How can such a thing be called pride? Simple. Both pride and false humility are self-absorbed. It is more socially acceptable than its counterpart, but just as damaging to the building of godly character. This subtle power works to turn our attention from God and His Word toward our failures, inabilities, and weaknesses. The result is that real faith is destroyed, because real faith is focused on God. Because false humility can work in secret, it should be feared above its sibling.

Pride doesn't just die of old age, either. It won't go away, even if it's denied or resisted. It cannot be controlled, and it will not be silent. It must be killed—crucified is the biblical term. Obedience to God is the simplest way to keep pride where it belongs—on the Cross. And obedience is first seen in changing the way we think. We are to believe and confess what God says…about anything. Walking in faith is a living testimony of crucified pride.

Can you believe it? The pride of some people…Dave actually considered himself, if only for a moment, to be a better fly fisherman than me.

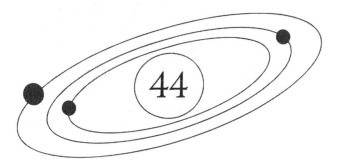

FORGIVENESS

One year the salmon were running in record numbers. I started taking quite a few pre-sunrise trips to the river to *partake of the harvest*. It was great fun, and after awhile I thought that my family should join me. I wanted my boys, who were about 8 and 10 at the time, to hook into one of these big silver fish. So on a beautiful summer evening, we went to one of the places that I had been frequenting on those early morning excursions. My boys and I had caught many bass and trout together, but salmon was going to be a new experience.

When we drove up to the hole, there were only a few people fishing. That was good. We were easily able to find a place to stand and cast our lines. Salmon fishermen are usually the most tolerant fishermen in the world. We'll stand shoulder to shoulder, by the hour, with little complaint. It must be the size of the fish that makes such conditions so acceptable. The strip of water that usually accommodated four to six fishermen was only hosting one elderly woman. We excitedly walked up to the hole and cast our lines into the water. Eric quickly hooked and landed a nice salmon. As soon as he did so, the woman spoke up. "I know what you guys are doing!" She then accused us of crowding her so that she couldn't catch anything. My first thought was, "You've got to be kidding! You ought to be here early in the morning!" We were about 15 to 20 feet away from her, which in salmon fishing terms is really far. Instead I stood silent, and thought about what she had said.

Did we crowd her? No. We kept a greater distance from her than normal. Besides, she couldn't have cast to the fish that Eric caught. Did she think we had crowded her? Yes. Was she offended? Yes. I suppose that I could have explained how things work on the river, streamside etiquette and all, but she didn't seem too interested in being told anything by me. We had just caught *her* fish. Instead I chose to set an example for my boys on how to show respect to our "elders" by giving up that whole stretch of river for her to enjoy. As we packed up our gear I apologized for offending her. She then apologized for her words and attitude, to which I answered, "I forgive you." This set off another visible reaction, though she managed to gather her thoughts and say in return, "And I forgive you."

Those are words that are too seldom spoken: "I forgive you."

I've had several devastating crises throughout my life. In each situation, which lasted from several months up to a couple of years, I was forced to discover the power and place of the walk of forgiveness in my life. And in each case I was to learn it with members of the Body of Christ.

Why is it that the three worst times of my life were caused, at least in part, by other Christians? The reasons are too numerous for the time and space allotted here, but to sum it up bluntly, God uses our imperfections to bring others to perfection, and visa versa.

Some have pointed to similar circumstances as proof that the Church is filled with hypocrites. But that approach only leads to further troubles. Unless we learn to live the life of a forgiver, we interpret every conflict through the eyes of our most recent crisis, infecting the rest of the Body of Christ with our bitterness.

I can approach an issue of forgiveness with one of two questions; "What do they owe me?" or "What do I owe them?" The question I ask will determine whether or not I forgive them. If I think about what they owe me, I'll walk in resentment. The one who is supposed to love me with the love of Christ has hurt me. But, if I consider what I owe them, I remember what it means that I have been forgiven by God. My gratitude and joy for His grace is to move me to extend that grace to anyone in need. The apostle Paul said, *"Owe no one anything except to love one another..."* (Rom. 13:8). We are debtors. We owe forgiveness, an evidence of real love.

There is one Christian who is harder to forgive than any other. Yourself! Why is it that a person who would never consider holding a grudge against someone else, holds himself in the prison of unforgiveness over something that is forgiven by God? Bitterness poisons our lives. It also has an effect on the person we are bitter toward. Thus, when we don't forgive ourselves, we get a double dose of the *fruit of bitterness.* And perhaps the most tragic part is that people allow themselves to fall into the trap of unforgiveness under the pretext of maintaining "high standards." We must not allow the enemy to use our desire for righteousness as a platform to convince us that not forgiving ourselves is noble. If you find yourself saying, "I'm proving my remorse for what I have done wrong," watch out! It's a trap!

How do we forgive ourselves? If forgiveness is releasing someone from a debt, then we must release ourselves from the debt of our past, and more importantly, no longer think of ourselves as the people we were. After all, who are you to refuse to forgive a member of the Body of Christ? That includes forgiving yourself! You are government property of the Kingdom of God. So handle with care!

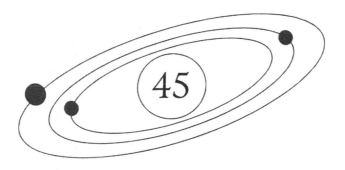

BRACES AND BASEBALL

It's reported that all orthodontists plug into the Ortho-Think Tank via the Internet. It's located somewhere in the jungles of Africa. This group of Teeth Generals work to discover ways to get back at the human race by figuring out how to legally torture us. They have worked for decades at perfecting this trade.

I think these professionals must slip something into the water to slightly anesthetize the unsuspecting public. How else can you account for something actually coming to me and saying, "I think you look good with braces." No one, and I mean no one, who looks like they tangled with a stainless steel freight train can look good. Almost mockingly these professional torturers ask me, when I go in for my monthly checkup, "Are you ready for brighter color ties?" (For those of you living the blessed life of ignorance, ties are the extremely small rubber bands that keep the wire connected to the metal that is glued to the teeth.) My response is always the same: "Give me the radical gray." And now I ask you the most logical question that comes to mind. If the metal sculpture protruding from one's mouth is ugly, why would one want to draw attention to it with fluorescent colored ties? Isn't it bad enough that when people stare at the metal in your mouth instead of your eyes, you wonder if there might be a piece of lettuce wrapped around your wires? Why would anyone want to place the oral equivalent of neon lights on their teeth? And yet, all over the country, people are walking out of their orthodontist's offices with chartreuse, hot pink, and other colors appropriate only for steelhead lures hooked to every tooth. I'm telling you, something has been put in the water.

I understand that rubber bands are used to help move teeth, the jaw, and through personal experience, one's food. I happen to have a band that goes across the front of my teeth, diagonally from top to bottom, thus requiring removal before eating. And if I forget? I'll remember soon enough! Last week I was going to eat a small rice cake covered in caramel. I tossed it into my mouth. It never touched my lips, but landed back in my hand. For a brief moment I thought this little cake had a mind of its own, refusing to be eaten. Then I remembered the rubber bands. This morning I placed a candy mint in my mouth. It seemed to fight back. When I opened my mouth the mint flew out onto the floor, much like a grasshopper escaping the clutches of a hungry bird. It is strange what passes through a person's mind in the millisecond following such a strange event.

The worst thing about braces, not counting the pain, or ugliness, or cost, is the fact that *you can't take them off* when they're inconvenient and put them back on when all is well. But, the best thing about braces is that *you can't take them off* when they are inconvenient. Really, braces are like devoted, faithful teachers…teachers who will not change the subject no matter how much discomfort I'm in, and no matter how much I feel humiliated. The very thing I hate about them is the very thing I love. Because they don't quit, my teeth have moved into place.

This past week I watched Cal Ripkin break the record of consecutive games played by a Major League Baseball player, with 2,131 games. I believe it covered something like 14 seasons. Around 80 other shortstops (his position) have come and gone during this time. He remains. I believe this is to be *the greatest single record in all of sports,* bar none. I honestly fought to hold back tears as I watched this event unfold. I have been anticipating that day for several years. The standing ovation that the Baltimore Oriole fans gave him lasted for over 22 minutes. The fans in other baseball stadiums around the country gave him standing ovations when the news of his record was broadcast over their loudspeakers.

What made this record possible? He was blessed physically, never having been seriously injured. He was blessed with a level of skill that made him an asset to his team long after others his age had been forced to retire. Neither of those things was entirely in his control. Then what makes this record so great? It is because of the one thing he could control—his heart, the seat of his character. The trait needed for this accomplishment, and the one I value most in people, is *faithfulness.* Annoying injuries or personal problems that take one's mind off the task at hand commonly work to remove people from their responsibilities in life. It's the rare heart that keeps a person going when others have quit.

I once knew a woman who could be called the *Cal Ripkin* of the Kingdom of God— Mrs. Dambacher, now home with the Lord. She faithfully taught a Sunday school class for 2-year-olds for close to 40 years. During this time she was dirt poor and hunchbacked from scrubbing floors to help make ends meet, all while being married to a rebellious, cantankerous old man who mocked her love for God. Her generosity was amazingly similar to the woman of Scripture who gave all she had. Her joy was contagious. She was a rare heart. I can only imagine that her standing ovation, that thunderous approval given to her by the *"crowd of witnesses"* (Heb. 12:1), will only be overshadowed by the shout of the Master saying, "Well done, good and faithful servant."

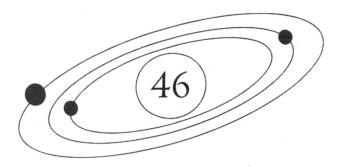

Hunting in the Good Old Days

Grandpa Morken used to love to talk of the old days...the days that would never be again. And I loved to listen. My favorite stories were the ones about hunting and fishing in Minnesota during the earlier part of this century. That is the state in which most of my family was born.

Many stories centered on his dog named Joe. Joe was a cocker spaniel, a natural hunter who had never been trained. He would get excited whenever Grandpa would go to the gun cabinet. Joe knew that the gun meant hunting, and hunting meant pleasure.

Although he would swim seemingly halfway around the world to recover the duck that was down, pheasant was his specialty. And the cold that is synonymous with hunting in Minnesota didn't seem to bother him.

Joe ate only table scraps. They never bought him dog food. Things were different then. This seemed to be a point that came up often in Grandpa's stories.

I loved it when he would pull out the old black and white pictures of large whitetail deer, many of them, hanging on large poles, in cold-looking deer camps. Standing next to them were the hunters, most of whom were relatives of mine. And then there were the pictures of the rows of ducks or pheasants laid neatly before the front bumper of a car. The proud hunters stood alongside their prey, recording the memories for future generations to enjoy.

The stories of fishing were equally exciting. Being the land of over 10,000 lakes, the fishing was close to supernatural. At least at the age of 10, I couldn't imagine Heaven to be greater than lakes and fish, everywhere.

I was able to visit Minnesota when I was around 11. Anticipating such a trip can be similar to the anxiety of a child on Christmas Eve. My mother's uncle said he'd take me fishing. He not only promised that we would catch fish, he said he'd give me $5 if we didn't—a large sum of money then. We caught many, many fish. Just as I thought; I *had* died and gone to Heaven.

Grandpa was not an exaggerator. Among outdoorsmen this is rare. If many of my acquaintances tell me they caught an 18-inch trout, I picture one about 14 inches long. If Grandpa said it was 18 inches long, it would have been exactly 18 inches, or perhaps 18 and a little more. If he said it happened a certain way, you could *take it to the bank*. He was a man of God first, a sportsman later.

I often regretted that I hadn't lived 40 years sooner. It was such a simple day then. Hunting had so little opposition. And the opportunities were abundant. It seemed a shame to have missed that golden opportunity. I was born a generation or two too late.

Being of a modern era, I recently glanced over the long list of hunting and fishing shows in my satellite television guide and noticed one on pheasant hunting. Being the proud owner of a German Shorthair Pointer, I have taken an even greater interest in this fine bird imported from China. I set my VCR to the appropriate time. When I sat down and watched the show I was somewhat shocked by what I saw. The narrator informed me that there had been two great periods of time, during this century, for hunting pheasants in the United States. One was in the '30s (my grandfather's era), and the other in the '60s. I was alive and hunting during that time. I didn't bother to hunt pheasant much. The days of *great hunting* were over, or so I thought. Grandpa never taught me that...but somehow I learned it.

Prime pheasant hunting, the kind that men write about, *was* within reach. I now have been left to read what others have written, instead of writing of it myself. I was so convinced of the best being in the past, that I missed the chance to experience it for myself. Pheasant hunting has no eternal significance, unless we listen and allow the natural to teach us of the spiritual.

We in the church are very prone to this kind of mistake. Unfortunately it has to do with more than just birds. The mistake is an overall negativity about life on this planet. For example, we have a common understanding that *darkness will cover the earth*. From our view, things will get worse and worse, *then the end will come*. The problem that I see with this kind of thinking is that it is very appealing to the *religious flesh*. In other words, it is easy to come to that conclusion apart from real faith. That alone should warn us of potential problems.

It's not a question of whether or not bad things will happen. The Bible is clear on that. But what we sometimes miss is what God is going to do that will give the *Kingdom alternative* to the impending darkness. Isaiah 60:1-2 is a good example, *"Arise, shine; for your light has come! And the glory of the Lord is risen upon you. For behold, the darkness shall cover the earth, and deep darkness the people; but the Lord will arise over you, and His glory will be seen upon you."* It's obvious to see that there are two things happening—the tragedy, and God's antidote. One requires faith to experience, and the other requires nothing.

I'm ready if we happen to have another pheasant heyday. I'll not be looking at photos wishing that I had lived 60 years ago. But even if that day never comes, there's one heyday that I plan *not* to miss. Proverbs 4:18 declares, *"The path of the just is like the shining sun, that shines ever brighter unto the perfect day."* Haggai the prophet said, *"The glory of the latter house will be greater than the former"* (Hag. 2:9 KJV). We are the house, and this is the day. It's Prime Time!

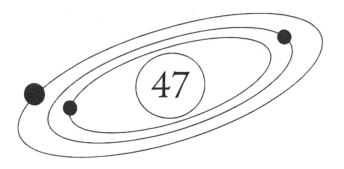

LOVING THE UNDESERVING

My family and I sat around the table this morning eating breakfast and having our devotions. As I was reading to them out of Proverbs, this verse seemed to stand out, *"The righteous is concerned for the rights of the poor, the wicked does not understand such concern"* (Prov. 29:7 NASB). So I asked them if it would be right to feed poor people who came to us in need, but also told us of their marijuana plants or other assorted sins. Their answer was, "Yes." Jesus loved us while we were sinners. We are to do the same.

We are often torn with the story of a good family that has faced tragedy. Many times a community will rally around such a family and give to them according to their need. It has been a privilege for all of us to participate in such projects. But if the town drunk faces a calamity or someone of questionable character, they are often cast to the winds of fate. When Solomon mentioned that the wicked don't understand such concern, he was referring in part to this scenario. Jesus said to love our enemies. Why? Anyone can show mercy to a friend. It's the obviously undeserving—in our eyes—whom we must concentrate upon. Our love for them is the proof of our conversion.

The world is not opposed to helping the poor. Quite the opposite. The world just doesn't like helping those who deserve their calamity or those who might be taking advantage of them. Jesus never had such a worry. He simply loved everyone in a way that was best for them.

While I would never want to imply that all the misfortunate are poor because of their own sins, it is the case of most who come to us for food and other physical needs. And I must say it is quite releasing not to be concerned over whether or not they are taking advantage of us. We overlook their lack of personal hygiene, or even yet ignore the fact that they might be lying (how can you get to Weaverville from Sacramento while driving to Phoenix?).

Remember, for each of us it was undeserved love that has forever changed our lives.

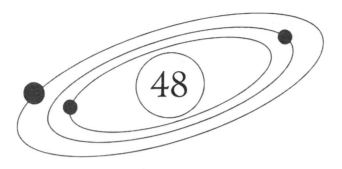

TP

It was late in the day, and we were lacking one of the more essential provisions of life—TP. Many young people use this commodity to dedicate their friend's homes and trees. Backpackers call it *mountain money*, and for good reason. When you lack this item while hiking you consider all your worldly goods as a fair trade for a single roll. If you still don't know what I'm talking about, here's another hint—some brands are *squeezably soft*.

Eric was kind enough to go to the store and buy a pack for our household (which is the real reason that God puts it in the heart of young people to want to drive—errands!). He came home with a real deal. Something like 4,000 rolls for a nickel (slight exaggeration). It was obvious to all that he was pleased with his wise purchase.

It's amazing how many things can flash through your mind in that millisecond when you realize that you've neglected an important area of instruction in raising your children. You see, I had never told Eric about buying toilet paper before. I held the mega-roll package in my hands, fearing the worst. I then read those horrible words...*single ply*. And to make matters worse, it was generic. I'm somewhat embarrassed to say this, but I had about a three-minute period of time where I was in a semi-controlled state of panic, trying to figure out how I was going to return the magnum package without hurting my son's feelings about being a wise consumer, and probably look like a fool at the store. In that brief moment I recalled how I used to state emphatically to the few who would listen, that single-ply toilet paper was from the antichrist. I had always felt somewhat guilty about talking of something so serious in such a shameless fashion and recently dropped that point from my theology.

After I had regained my composure, I began to explain to Eric the difference between one- and two-ply, realizing that he had never even seen the *one* in our home. After a brief moment of instruction, (a sermon, in his mind), I accepted the fact that we were actually going to use this product. Eric listened to my words intently, as any responsible son would, and tried hard to get a feel for where my heart was. His response? "Dad, you're funny. You are FUNNY!" And we all had a good laugh, until I realized that they were all laughing at me. In a house full of comedians, I am the inspiration for their material.

I would never say that God caused this situation, lest you write me off of your *sanity list* for good…and lest you think, "Does he really believe that this is a problem? I wish I had it so good." But I can promise you this: while God didn't cause it, He enjoyed it immensely! God probably gave Eric a standing ovation. I doubt that He has ever needed to use toilet paper in someone's life as a way to reveal his or her heart before…until now. He probably still has a slight grin on His face from the whole incident. Why? Does toilet paper actually matter to God? Nope, not in the least! The problem is it mattered that much to me.

Why is it that I believe God actually got involved in this? Because of what went through my mind in that brief moment immediately after opening the bag. You see, I had been studying discipleship again and was reviewing the cost of being a true believer. I had recently been to Mexico and was reminded of how the average person lives there. Personal sacrifice was fresh on my mind. I was geared up and ready to live sacrificially in any area that I had overlooked. I opened the bag, saw the inevitable, and my first thought was, "Now this has gone too far. You want me to use single-ply toilet paper? This is ridiculous! I've got standards, you know. Now, this *can't* be God!" When you find yourself defending the indefensible, shut up and listen. He's probably trying to say something.

In order to follow Christ, we forsake all. We've given up sleep, just to help someone. We've given possessions and money to serve a person worse off than we are. At times, even our health has been put at risk because of our attempts to follow the sacrificial example that Jesus gave to us. Jesus does not work in me so that He can have my money, goods, or even my time. He works to have my heart. Period. And it's a strange experience to see how many meaningless things can be attached to a heart. Of course, anything in life is meaningless in comparison to knowing God. The real embarrassment comes when I see that I have something so dear to my heart that is so meaningless to the rest of the planet.

I'm happy to say that two-ply is back in my house. But after seeing the TP job that had been done in my heart, it's not quite as serious an issue. I'm well aware of how God dealt with some of His prophets and am a little concerned that He might bless my household with a large stack of Sears catalogues. And I guarantee you, it wouldn't take me long to sing the praises of *single-ply*.

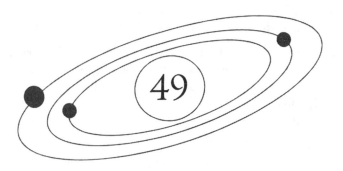

WHO WE ARE

Often people make comparisons between churches, such as Mountain Chapel versus the one they've come from, or possibly visited. Sometimes we look pretty good, and other times we come up short. We are graded according to how we do in the areas that are important to that particular *fruit inspector.* It's impossible to prevent this from happening; I have my favorites too. Yet I would prefer that we not be compared with those who don't walk in the truth that God has required of us, or with those who have received an insight that God has withheld from us. God is the One who reveals truth. And He sometimes chooses to give insights to one church and not to another. (This applies to individuals too.) He is the Sovereign One. At times He deliberately keeps insight from us to test our response to those who grow where we are weak.

If we compare ourselves with the churches that accomplish more than us, we are left to discouragement and low faith. If we are compared with those who do not practice what we feel is priority, there is the unavoidable opportunity for pride. And neither discouragement nor pride will help us. Obedience to the call is the only thing that will satisfy the heart's cry for achievement.

While I steer away from comparing ourselves with others, I do believe that every local church has a unique twist to their emphasis and call. If that be the case, what are the things that make us different? The following are just some of the issues that God has placed His italics on for us.

Worship. Worship has been priority #1 for at least 16 years. It is who we are, not just what we do. We are not focused on performance; it is relationship-centered. Worship takes a large segment of our time together, much to the dismay of Christians who were raised under a different set of values. Seldom do you find a believer who would say worship is unimportant. Our distinction is to minister to God with the expressions taught in the Psalms, sometimes referred to as Davidic Worship; they are verbal and physical.

Ministry. Everyone is a minister. Everyone has at least one gift in which they can excel. With it we are to honor God, bring strength to the Body of Christ, and make the Gospel visible to the world. Each person has been created in the image of God. No one represents God in the same way as another; we are special! Every person knows instinctively that God has created them for significance. This is discovered in ministry—service.

City of Refuge. This city has a call from God, which in turn means that all its citizens have complementary gifts. God has promised to bring people from all over the world for healing. (It has been pronounced. Therefore, watch out for the enemy's counterfeit.) Broken people will find their way here and receive restoration. Fallen leaders in the church will come because we accept them without judgment. They will be nurtured back to spiritual health. Even now people of all walks of life are brought to this city, many of whom do not know the Lord. Yet God planned their steps and ordained that they would learn of His salvation here. This call is embryonic in its present form but will be realized more in the near future.

Infiltrate the System. This is a call to service. The Kingdom of God has been compared to leaven in Scripture. Leaven is worked into dough quietly, without fanfare. From its strategic placement, it influences everything it touches. So it is with the church. We have been sprinkled, like salt, into this community. We are not here to rule. We are here to serve. From this place of service—our place of strength—people come to Christ. Because of this mandate, we pray, plan, and pursue opportunities to be sprinkled into the system.

World Ministry. We are called to the nations. This call is strong. It has been of God's design that we train young people as well as adults for short-term service in world missions. All can go. All must participate in some fashion. This call goes against the grain of America's small community. It has been commonly thought that big cities or big churches do big things. And anyone who will cooperate with Him will be used in what He considers significant. Missions was never meant to be left to the *professional*. This vision grows out of the belief that nothing is impossible with God. He uses the foolish things to confound the wise, the small things to challenge the big, and the unimpressive to touch the elite. God, plus one willing servant, is a majority!

We have walked in each of these areas, yet none of them is complete or mature. Diligence and faithfulness will bring us into further maturity. There is probably a simpler way to express all of this. Perhaps saying, "Know and love God, reach far and wide, and don't forget the last chapter—we win!" would suffice.

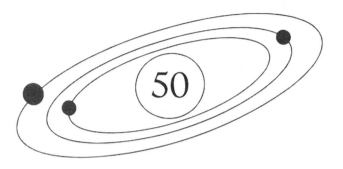

BEATITUDES

To be truly happy, you must be aware of your spiritual needs. One must know what sorrow is, be gentle and humble, hungry for goodness above all else, a giver of mercy, pure in thought and motive, a worker to bring peace, and one who suffers for doing what is right without taking revenge.

The results of these attitudes are: having the prized possession of God's Kingdom, being comforted whenever there is a difficulty, becoming the heir of God's earth, having your desires fulfilled, being treated with mercy by others, an ongoing revelation of God, having others recognize you as a child of God, and living under the lordship of Jesus with the awareness of an eternal reward.

The previous two paragraphs are a personal paraphrase of the Beatitudes from the Sermon on the Mount. I put it in print to place on my office wall as a reminder of the mind of Christ.

Many would claim that Jesus isn't concerned about our happiness. He is. But keep in mind He knows there's only one way to find it—His way! The Bible is filled with the lesson of reaping and sowing, cause and effect. First there is the attitude, then there is the effect (reward) of the attitude. And that reward is the ultimate description of happiness. From inheriting the earth to an ongoing revelation of God. From the comfort of friends to an eternal reward. True happiness!

Read it with personal reflection. It is difficult to work at getting the favor of others, but I can work on the attitude in me with a result of an increase of such favor. Wouldn't it be great for someone to say of us, "He/she's got an attitude," referring to the mind of Christ?

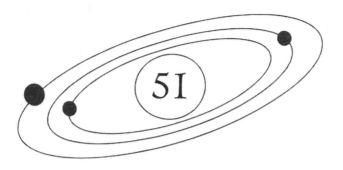

REPENTANCE

Wouldn't you know it? I teach against jealousy one Sunday, and have the privilege of repenting for it before the next.

I saw that ugly monster rise within my heart when I heard of a fallen individual being restored at another church. You see, years ago he met the Lord with us. It's not that I wasn't happy for his return to Christ. I was very happy! It's that I felt cheated. No words were spoken against him or the church. But when I saw it in my heart, I had to quickly repent. Perhaps that's why Paul called it the *"fight of faith"* (1 Tim. 6:12). Sometimes it requires all the fight that I have.

Why would jealousy be the response of my heart when hearing of such great news? I must admit if it weren't so repulsive, it would appear silly. Through some soul-searching, I've come to see that there still remains in me some of the world's influence of competition and competitiveness ("my church").

So what do we do when the Holy Spirit reveals more of the "not so good, the bad, and the ugly" in us? First is confession. That word means to agree with God. He says it's ugly and wrong and we say Amen! Second is to forsake the sin. This is done by obeying God's Word on the subject, which in this case requires me to prefer (see Rom. 12:10) my brother (or church) over myself. So in prayer I asked for the blessing of the Lord on that great flock of God and upon my restored brother. Third, we must be renewed in our mind by the Word of God (see Rom. 12:2). This means that I must accept my forgiveness and not wallow in guilt. It also means that I must consider myself dead to sin (see Rom. 6:11). The reality of that statement is that through the gift of God's atonement, sin is no longer my commander and chief.

Jealousy is like all other sin. It's born out of pride and unbelief. Let's not allow the enemy to rob us of the beauty of being "one body" through such sin. Confess, forsake, and rejoice in the liberty of the renewed mind.

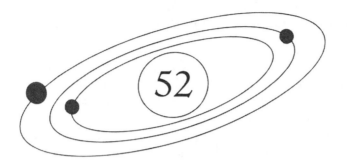

THE DAY THE FREEZER DIED

Trash stinks. Especially old trash. But the worst smelling of all was the stuff we didn't know was trash.

There was a strange odor coming from the workshop next to the carport. This was nothing new. We keep our trash out there and sometimes I let it age.

A day or so after sending my boys to the dump with the garbage, I went out by the shop...whew! When I talked to one of them that evening I made the following sermon short and simple. It was something like, "You need to look for all the bags of trash so that you can do the job well." I thought it was a good sermon, especially for a short one. They thought they got it all, but agreed to go again.

When we came home from church last week, a couple of days after my exhortation on dump runs, we were hit by a wall of smell. Now, unless the following has happened to you, to imagine this smell is almost impossible. We opened the car doors and wished we were at the wrong address. It was more than a bag of trash. Something was *dead*.

As we got closer to the workshop, the smell became as close to physical as imaginable. We walked into the little room and were greeted by about a zillion flies, newly born, and a smell that abused all senses. In that moment of truth, we realized that our freezer had died. And worse yet, all the dead things inside were the soil for new beginnings; it was teeming with new forms of life. To describe in detail what we saw inside would garner an "R" rating. I not only almost lost my breakfast, I almost lost all of last week's breakfasts, as well as the ones yet to come. My sons had taken all the trash to the dump, as they told me. Oops.

We had come home to pack for a week of meetings at the Redwood Family Camp, where I was to speak. As usual, we were in a hurry. How do you take care of such a problem in a few minutes? The dump was closed. And there is no listing in the yellow pagers for *Removers of Dead Things from Dead Freezers.* So I called for help. Buck Steele, who is swamped with work, came to my rescue. Servants do that.

Beni and I double-packed a decaying bear hide (once intended for a rug), newly hatched Cornish game hens (from their plastic wrappers), salmon, trout, venison, and other UDOs (Unidentified Dead Objects), in plastic bags so that he could take both the freezer and the decomposed flesh to the dump. On Monday morning Buck and our son Eric (who stayed home for American Legion Baseball), took our offering to the dump. Eric said he's never heard Buck laugh so hard.

Although I wasn't there, I have imagined all the other trash getting up and moving, not wanting to associate with my trash. And if banana peels and old newspapers could write, I would be receiving hate mail. As it is, I don't want to go back to the dump for several months, just in case they know who I am. A dump revolt must be the worse possible uprising.

How do flies get into closed freezers? It doesn't seem possible. They have a way of finding death and multiplying at a frightening rate. Decaying flesh seems to be their favorite meal, and even open wounds on the living will attract them.

All of this seems to shed a little light on the nature of the most disgusting creature of all—satan. He is called beelzebub, meaning lord of the flies. That is a name Jesus gave to the devil. A suitable name to be sure.

The nature of flies and the nature of the devil are so similar. They both love death. They are both attracted to and love to feast on the open wounds of humanity. And wherever there is death that is left untended, no matter how securely hidden away it seems to be, they both find it and multiply their efforts.

People place value in the strangest things. We could never imagine someone holding on to my *bags of meat* as a valued treasure. Yet often people will hold on to the tragedies of yesterday with a similar *fatal attraction.* What is it about humankind that would cause people to hide bitterness away in their hearts as though they actually had something of value? And if the sin of bitterness wasn't bad enough by itself, the flies come and multiply with beelzebub reigning as lord of that situation.

Why would anyone not want to confess the hidden sins of the heart to the One who forgives all who come to Him? It would seem like the logical thing to do, unless one likes to stink.

Do you have BO, as in the odor of flesh (carnality—our nature apart from Christ) and sin? The alternative is the fragrance that comes from brokenness…like the smell of our worship. It is very pleasing to God. He loves the intercessions—prayers—of the saints. They are as incense before Him. We also are the fragrant aroma of Christ to God. A revelation of how God smells wouldn't hurt any of us.

Now thanks be to God who always leads us in triumph in Christ, and through us diffuses the fragrance of His knowledge in every place. For we are to God the fragrance of Christ among those who are being saved and among those who are perishing (2 Corinthians 2:14-15).

Do you have a broken freezer filled with unwanted surprises? Confession and repentance are the only known Odor-Eaters!

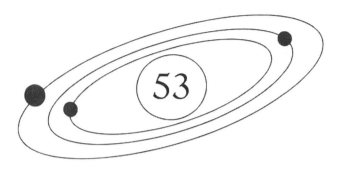

CYNICISM

While doing some writing this morning, I needed to know how to spell "cynicism." I have a "cheater box." I type the word into it and push a button and it tells me if I spelled it right. If I didn't, I push another button and it prints out the way I'm supposed to spell that word. The only problem is, you can't be a bad speller. It only works for those who are just sort of bad. So I typed my version of the word—synisism. It responded, "Say what?" I'm not kidding. This gadget laughed at me. It said back, "Are you trying to spell 'syntactic'?" Oh, now that's a word I use every day.

This "word finder" has another wonderful feature. It gives synonyms. Being as curious as I am, I pushed the appropriate button. It said, "None found." Right, just as I thought. Syntactic is not a word. This machine is only here to bring me into confusion. Well, back to my word. This time I typed in synasism. It printed back "synapses" (not synopsis). I thought, *What does that word mean?* You guessed it, "None found." I tried cynasism. Its response, "Are you trying to spell 'cynosure'?" Sure. Webster tells me that's an old name for the "constellation of Ursa Minor" and definitely was not on my mind. Finally I came across a version it recognized, synicism. Bingo.

I was humiliated, only because I wanted to tell you how cynicism is the enemy of faith. It causes people to gamble, "What have I got to lose?" Young people lead immoral lives and toy with the prospect of AIDS, saying, "We're all going to die anyway." The bumper sticker says, "Question Authority," and our news commentators tell us that every decision of a politician is only to improve his public image. All of this is because of cynicism, or should I say, unbelief. Cynicism leads us into risk. Faith leads to the rock...God Himself. He is absolute and without risk.

By the way, syntactic means "in accordance with the rules of syntax." Would you believe I knew it all the time? I didn't think so.

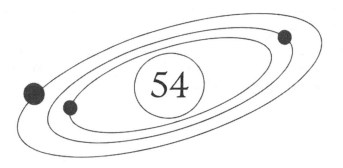

My Wedding Ring

I had my wedding ring cut off today. It seems that either gold shrinks when wet or I must have had it surgically grafted onto my finger on our wedding day. The jeweler told me to come back in two weeks to see what size ring I really wear. She said it would take that long for the strangled part of my finger to come to its full size again. Beni said she was surprised that it hadn't cut off the circulation. It really wasn't that tight. But it did remind me of a ship in a bottle.

I remember the last time I had taken the ring off. It was in 1979. Another pastor and I were returning from a conference in Atlanta, Georgia, when our 727 lost an engine somewhere between Denver and San Francisco. We had to make an emergency landing in Reno. The flight attendants were frantically running up and down the aisles giving us instructions on how to prepare ourselves for our unusual landing. We were told to remove all pens from our pockets, glasses from our faces, watches from our wrists, and rings from our fingers. No problem. Until I got to the ring. I told her that it wouldn't come off. She insisted, saying that it must. So I licked and spit and finally pulled off a trick that would have impressed Houdini himself. I felt like telling her that if I survived a crash landing (somehow those two words shouldn't go together—either you land or you crash) and lost my finger because I left my ring on, I wouldn't be mad. I promise. But I got it off before I found the courage.

We were then given pillows to put on our laps, and told to bury our heads in it with our arms wrapped around our legs in a fetal position. This was quite uncomfortable for reasons I'll not explain, except to say, don't ever drink much coffee or anything else if you think you're going to have a crash landing. The other pastor and I got the giggles. He shared the same feelings of discomfort as I. As we got prepared to "land," we couldn't hold our heads down any longer. When we looked out the window we saw the fire trucks that lined the runway, red lights flashing, and ambulances prepared for the worst. We landed without the crash.

Since that eventful day, the ring has stayed on my finger, until now. It is being enlarged. I'd like to think it's because our love continues to grow. But some of you probably think it's me that's getting bigger. Nah!

SUCCESS

Who doesn't want to be a success? If someone didn't, I'm afraid that I wouldn't want to hang around him or her. People with ambition and desire are encouraging to be with... sometimes. That is, if they don't run you over first. Even then we tend to admire them for their "get up and go."

The desire for success is born of God. But that doesn't mean that all desire is born of God. It just means that the basic need to achieve is from our Father. So what is success?

One man works beyond what is normally expected and earns his doctorate. Another quits right before reaching that hard-earned goal. He says it's because God required it from him.

One woman goes against the tide to become a skilled attorney, and another abandons her law practice to join the Peace Corps.

An accomplished athlete signs a multimillion-dollar contract for his services, while another uses his "mega-buck" skills to travel the world with a Christian organization, preaching the gospel.

Of all these, who are the successful ones? Possibly all of them, and possibly none. We tend to measure success with dollar signs and numbers or personal satisfaction and religious-looking standards. God measures success with one word—obedience. It is possible to turn down the big contract, travel the world preaching the gospel, and still not be successful in God's eyes. That would be the route that would get you the most recognition for being sacrificial, but it's not necessarily the right thing to do. It might be in the Kingdom's best interest to be in the public's eye as a role model, making major dollars, quietly funding Christian ministries around the world, using status as a platform for the gospel. But again, only at God's command.

So what is success? It is to know Him, to obey Him, and to make Him known.

Be successful! K.I.S.S.! (Keep it simple, saint!)

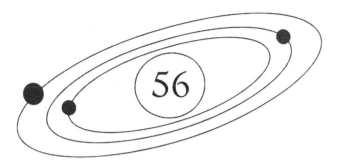

FACING IMMORALITY

KGO Radio recently announced a new plan by the police department of San Francisco. They are now going to make it illegal for prostitutes to sell themselves on specific city streets. It seems that the citizens of those neighborhoods complained about the dangers that are posed to their children because of the activities of these women (and men). The prostitutes are going to protest.

Excuse me, but isn't prostitution illegal on *any* street?

When city hall declares that an illegal activity will not be allowed in certain areas of town, they are saying that it will be allowed in others. And we wonder why it's hard to enforce our laws.

Our soon-to-be President is planning to keep two election promises—abortion becoming a constitutional right and homosexuality being acceptable in the military. Without a "Damascus Road" experience, these will no doubt happen after the first of the year. Watch and see—President Clinton will be recognized for financial integrity and compassion for those in need. Why? Immorality must be clothed with morality to be justified and swallowed by the American people.

We must accept responsibility for this moral deficit. The generation that was afraid to spank because it could not damage their children's self-esteem now says, "Abstinence is best, but here's a condom and a birth-control pill"—another life-changing message from the Radical Middle—a spineless declaration!

So now what? First, we must be well-established in God's Word, not just in conservative rhetoric. Second, we must know how to kneel and stand. We kneel to pray. We stand to speak.

In the midst of the outcry for more immoral liberties is a generation that looks for someone with backbone. Jesus had it, and it's hereditary. His backbone bent only to pray.

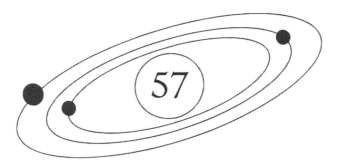

MISTAKES

This must be the hour of the recall. Citizens recall their elected officials and manufacturers recall their products.

Automobiles seem to top the list of durable goods that are recalled. What a hassle! Because they didn't do it right the first time, you have to make the trip to the dealership and lose a day or so just to get what you already paid for. Perhaps it was the air conditioner that wasn't functioning properly. Or maybe the seatbelt.

This morning's news carried the Mother of All Recalls. Pacemakers. Can you imagine? It's not like going in for a tune-up or getting your tires rotated. At first I laughed. Then I was a little embarrassed, but glad I was alone, when I realized how un-funny it was for those who have the "loose wire" imbedded in their chests. Over 100,000 people are walking around with these defective tickers. That scare can't help those folks who already have weak hearts.

Mistakes can be made by all of us. The guy who rebuilt my brother's engine did it improperly, and he's known for his good work. The great surgeon, the architect, and even world leaders—all are subject to error.

The blunders that are the easiest to avoid are those that result from carelessness. Whether it's an error in manufacturing or a moral indiscretion, we are never destined to failure. Simple care for the little things can prevent years of heartache.

We live at a time when blunders are more costly, and carelessness is on the rise. That's a deadly combination. An awareness of the times that we live in should provide the sober heart that is needed to avoid carelessness at all costs.

Mistakes are going to be made by all of us. I guess the trick is to make one that affects air conditioners and not pacemakers.

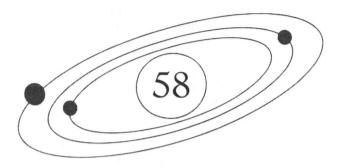

58

JUMPING TO CONCLUSIONS

For my birthday this past July, I was able to order a nice new rod for my favorite sport, fly-fishing. It was something I had dreamed about for quite some time. It was to be hand-built by a professional rod builder in Oregon. The drawback was that I would have to wait six to eight weeks. Oh well, I'm a patient guy.

August was soon over, and September was well underway, but no rod. Still being filled with patience, I called the shop in Oregon. I was assured it would be finished quickly and the concern was gone.

September and October are now gone, it's the middle of November, and not even a word about the rod. My patience still exists, but is slightly outweighed by concern. Before I call again, I start to wonder, *What if they are not in business anymore? My rod is paid for, and I'll be out all of that money.* I wonder if I'll have to "rejoice and give thanks" when I don't want to, again? When I called, an employee answered the phone, but couldn't answer my question. And the owner wasn't there. He took my number and assured me that the owner would get back to me in about an hour. But no call came. I called again, and the owner wasn't there. When I was asked to leave a message I "kindly" told him I had already tried that and was never called back, so I'd call again on my own.

During all this time, I was wondering if this wonderful fishing shop was still so wonderful. After all, the owner spent 20 minutes with me on the phone in July telling me about a new fishing reel he designed and how much money it was costing to develop. Maybe they went under. Would I have to go to small claims court to get my money back? Could I even get it back if he went bankrupt?

I wrote down the shop number so I could call from the office, but forgot to include the area code. When I finally got the Oregon area code, I called. And just like I suspected,

"The number you have called has been disconnected or is no longer in service." They went bankrupt! It all made sense now. I had that sneaking suspicion all along. And now I knew why. Besides, I should have known that ordering something so important over the phone was a mistake.

I decided that before I pressed charges, I should call my wife at home and have her check the phone number that I wrote down. It was correct all right, except for one small detail. It was an 800 number. Oops!

When I called the correct number, I talked with the owner, who was a real gentleman. He assured me that my rod was completed, and that he was waiting for a tube from the factory to ship it in (a very special tube). And to think, I almost had him bankrupt, in court, with many years of an excellent reputation down the drain. Have you ever jumped to conclusions only to wish you wouldn't have been so eager to jump? Me too.

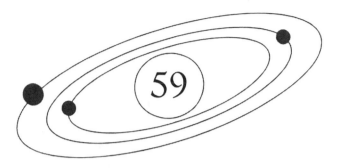

TEMPTATION

By the time you read this we will be facing some of the greatest temptations of our lives. Pray for Beni and me.

As many of you can attest, God's will sometimes takes us "into the wilderness to be tempted." It's not that God wants us to fail. Not at all! He just wants to reveal His good work in us, and where He still needs to heal and restore.

It's not enough that we will be faced with temptation; we will be confined to it. It's like being handcuffed to the very thing you're trying to get away from. Is it fair for anyone to go through such trial? And it's not just once a day. We will be faced with it seven times a day. Imagine, seven times a day, from sunrise to well after midnight.

You might wonder what is this cruel punishment that has befallen your pastor and his wife—three days on a cruise ship, with food being offered in seven different meals. I guess it's not too much of a wilderness experience, but it'll do in a pinch.

Kris and Kathy Vallotton won four tickets to a three-day cruise in the Bahamas. And they've invited us to share it with them. Being the loving pastor and wife that we are, we prayed much and decided to go. After all, they may need counsel or prayer, or at least help with all that food.

It's no secret that this has not been the easiest year of my life. Yet in the middle of it all, God's goodness far exceeds any problems. It's a wonder to me that in my most difficult year, He gives me a few days in Paris with my wife, and now the same on a ship with my wife and friends. Please take my testimony, and encourage yourself with it, remembering that the "testimony of Jesus is the spirit of prophecy." I can't promise you the Bahamas, but I can promise His faithfulness in the midst of trial.

By the way, your growing heart for God has healed mine. Thanks!

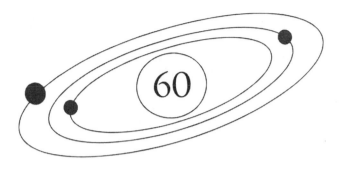

RESTORATION

"However, the hair of his head began to grow again..." (Judg. 16:22). This appears to be a rather strange Scripture to use as a key passage for any teaching, especially on the subject at hand. Yet contained in this verse is a beautiful revelation of God's nature as the Restorer. The verse, of course, is referring to Samson. He had fallen miserably. His lust for Delilah and his disrespect for the Nazarite vow brought great tragedy in his life. Worse yet, his sin brought suffering to Israel.

The Nazarite vow required them not to cut their hair or to partake of the fruit of the vine—wine, grapes, or even raisins. This was his assignment from God. He had disregard for the vow and lost the strength that God had given him by exposing his assignment to the whims of humankind. His strength was not his hair. It was God. And as long as his relationship with God was right, God was strong through him. He gave it all away through sin.

Even though there was destruction, even though many were hurt through his sin, "His hair began to grow again." Samson, the great judge of Israel, was humbled in the Philistine prison. It was after he lost everything that he realized all he had. His heart returned to his God, and he returned to his vow. Here is the greatness of the Lord—He restored his strength. The outcome is that there were more Philistines destroyed in Samson's final act of causing the temple of their false god to cave in, than in the rest of his life's exploits put together.

The lesson is simple—we must have a theology that sees God as the Restorer. And when He restores, it's often better than before the fall. This is our God, and He is great!

Again this week I've heard of more people who God is bringing back into the fold. More than at any other time I see this happening. Be involved in this mission—it's God assignment for us.

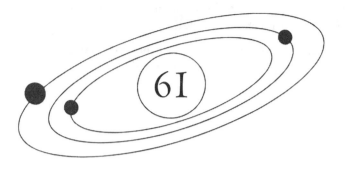

DISCIPLESHIP

I am a gadget person. I am fascinated with how things work, like computers or the latest pen. Typewriters and word processors are high on my list. My problem is that I don't understand how they work or how I can operate one. A picture comes to my mind of me sitting with this word processor, writing masterpieces, inspiring millions. Well, at least hundreds. While I am impressed with what they can do, I still don't know how they all work.

My problem goes back to yet another weakness. Instructions bother me. It doesn't matter whether it's on the back of a soup can or a manual for using a paper copier. I don't understand them. And worse than that, I get frustrated and abandon many a project because of this handicap.

This past month I finally put together a ceiling fan that was given to us almost two years ago. I lost the instructions, so I felt rather safe. When I came to a question of why the wires of my fan had different colors, I called Bob. He put his own together, and there's no voice like the voice of experience. He helped. It looked good and ready to mount, but...Because of the "but," it sat on my floor for about ten days. When the Vallottons came over to watch the 49ers dismantle the Redskins, Kris asked about my fan on the floor. He knew what it needed and we put it up—following the game, of course.

I honestly have a problem with instructions, to the point that Beni reads them to me slowly so I can grasp them. But when someone comes to help me who is experienced, I love to learn.

Many of us learn the Christian walk the same way. Only as someone shows us how to live do we really understand what is required of us. It's called discipleship. Find someone who lives like you want to live in Christ, and mimic that person. Ask questions of those you admire. Observe their behavior and learn.

While I do have a real difficulty with instruction manuals, etc., I rejoice that God always provides an example for those of us who really desire to grow.

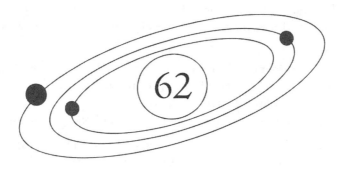

TRUE CONFESSION

Confessing sin has become a real art form. If you do it right, you can appear spiritual while admitting to sin. Phrases like, "The Holy Spirit has shown me..." or "God has been dealing with me about..." can emphasize our spirituality over our disobedience to God. It's another way of saying, "I have this tiny little sin—but through my deep devotion to God, and my sensitivity to His voice, I perceive that I have grieved Him. Therefore I confess...." It saves the horrible embarrassment of looking bad.

Another classic confession goes something like, "I need to confess the sin of a lack of discipline." Is the lack of anything sin? No. But it's a good way to confess the sin of laziness without using that ugly word and being humiliated.

If you want to be good at appearing spiritual while confessing sin, you'll have to ask yourself this question: "What will people think?" That is the driving force in the minds of ordinary people who overnight become masters of confession. Even those who haven't had a creative idea in years can rise to the challenge with that idea in mind. After all, looking good is the American way.

Let me illustrate some of the "how tos": If you find yourself nailed by God over stories that you've told that had slight embellishments in them, don't confess to *lying*. That's an extreme word and sounds much worse than "exaggeration." You could possibly try the suggestion of the previous paragraph and say, "I need to confess a sin. Because my memory isn't as good as it used to be, I am sometimes not as accurate in my stories as I should be." Or you could be bold and try the first suggestion, saying, "God has really been dealing with me lately. It seems that some of the stories that I've told had some slight exaggeration in them. Please forgive me." Either way, you save some face, without appearing like one of those habitual liars. And God only knows how many people would stumble if you made *that* admission.

One of the main goals of this kind of confession is to acknowledge sin without appearing like a sinner. That is, unless you are one of those who insists on walking out true repentance.

Solomon, in his wisdom, said, "He who is slothful in his work is brother to him who is a great destroyer." Can you imagine the lazy person saying, "Don't link my sin with that of terrorism. I just lack a little discipline." Protecting our self-image by going soft on sin is the sure way to damage our self-image and prolong our bondage to sinful habits.

I wish that I could say that I learned this from a book, but this is a page from my own life. Pride is the enemy of true confession. And real repentance is the destroyer of pride.

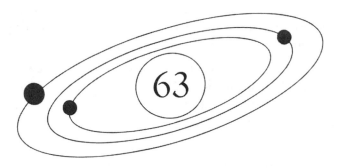

JOB'S FRIENDS

Job's life is one with which even the world is familiar. He is pitied for his suffering, his loss of wealth and family, and to top it off, the failure of his friends to give him the comfort he needed.

While Job's story has many lessons for us, it's the life of his associates that I find most intriguing. I won't stand in their defense—God rebuked them. On the other hand, I also don't want to be their accuser—they look too familiar.

Too often these guys are spoken of as disloyal, uncaring men. That is not completely true. In many ways they were caring, devoted, bright, and bold. Who else was even there when Job was in a crisis? Yet they missed the mark that God has set for us all.

In today's world, Job's friends would have made good theologians. Their understanding of God was noteworthy. They declared many wonderful truths in the counsel that they gave him. They were not dumb. It is evident from their discourses that they were men of great intellectual strength.

They also could fit nicely into the political arena with great success. Idealism, an absolute necessity for politicians, was their strong suit. And talking certainly came easy. They would probably be leaders both in the church and the community.

That same intellectual strength would have been of great help had they entered the medical profession. The amount of time that they spent with Job, attending to his needs and hoping for his recovery, was noble at the very least. Their compassion for the sick was evident in the way they put everything else aside just to care for him.

On the more humorous side I can see them as college professors. There are many in that profession who seem to fit the personal profile of these friends of Job—opinionated, without the much-needed practical experience in real life. But then, come to think of it, many pastors and religious leaders also speak from that position, teaching personal opinions as absolute truth.

Continuing in that frame of mind, I think their greatest contribution to humankind would have been as radio talk show hosts. With strong ideas and the ability to articulate, a large audience would almost be guaranteed. Can you imagine the hours of discussion they could have had with their open forum on *Did God Make Job Sick?*

On the other hand, they would have made great talk show guests! Can you see them on Oprah or Geraldo? "Rev. Donahue" probably would have given them the Humanist of the Year Award. Audiences would have likened them to Mother Teresa.

It's much easier to judge their lives from this side of history. Yet they did excel in many notable areas. In spite of all this, they still will always be known for what they lacked—the common sense for when to be quiet, which is an underestimated characteristic for good relationships.

They failed at being true friends. Friendship says, *My presence is more important than my words. My silence is as valuable as my insight. And my faithfulness is a gift that you don't have to earn.*

Many of the people who come to our churches don't realize that they need God. But they know that they are looking for friends. God knew that and filled us with His Holy Spirit. When we become friends, people get a little taste of God Himself. Since the Bible calls us "salt," guess Who they thirst for when we've been a true friend?

An important priority for us in this hour is the emphasis on being friends with people. It's somewhat humiliating to have to mention something so elementary. Yet we are surrounded by lonely people. Ironic, isn't it? Lonely people in the middle of a crowd.

Busyness is what most often prevents me from being all that I purpose to be. Like most, I have a life filled with good intentions. All too often those plans are devoured by good but less meaningful activities.

For 11 years I had planned on having Pastor Dan Tennyson and his family over for dinner. They are good friends and have been partners of ours in ministry to this city. Now that they have moved to pastor in Oregon, I am left with a memory of good intentions instead of a memory of good fellowship.

Seldom is there a day that goes by that I don't realize the importance of people over programs, and friendships over selfish pleasures. Yet seldom does a day go by that I don't somehow fail in the application of this all too important truth. It is so easy to put time into something that doesn't require my all. Friendship is certainly not that way. It is costly.

Continue to preach the gospel. Without hearing, people can never respond to God's gift of salvation. Just don't forget about the privilege of long-term evangelism—friendship.

Place a "Help Wanted" sign over your heart. The Holy Spirit will come and teach you the secret of being a real friend. He knows how. Remember, Jesus called Him *The Comforter.*

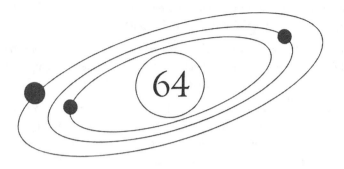

TRUE LOYALTY

What is loyalty? It is perhaps the most misunderstood virtue of all. The Bible says that, *"Many a man proclaims his own loyalty, but who can find a trustworthy man?"* (Prov. 20:6 NASB). What does that mean? To me it's saying that most people consider themselves to be loyal, but God says, "Not!"

That being the case, what is loyalty? A dog's master dies. The dog, considered to be man's best friend, goes to his grave and stays there. He ignores his need for companionship, and even his need for food. If he could, would he ask the question, "How can I prove my loyalty to my master?" Not hardly. Loyalty is not introspective—there's nothing to prove. Today's believer often works hard to prove existing character. A loyal heart just is.

A wife sees her husband fail in business. They were accustomed to a high standard of living. Now he's lost everything. Knowing that they will not be able to live the extravagant lifestyle they once enjoyed, he suggests that she return to her parents until he can rebuild his life and business. She reminds him that she was there when he had nothing, and that her love for him is not determined by what they possess. She stays with him and is able to rejoice in being part of the support that enabled him to succeed once again. Loyalty is not based on circumstances; it is directed toward people...period.

A young drug addict is converted. The pastor who worked the streets that day is devoted to him and converts the young man in the ways of the Lord. The new believer becomes strong, leading many others to Christ. They in turn grow with the same intensity, as kind reproduces kind. As the years go by, the responsibilities of the pastor and disciple take them to different parts of the country. One day, news of the now older pastor comes to the ex-addict. It is news of the most discouraging kind; there has been a moral failure in his spiritual hero. Who is left to care for him? His church fires him. His peers disown him. Yet there is a man who remembers that he owes his life to his "father in the faith." He seeks out the pastor, remains a friend, and is part of his restoration.

So what is loyalty? From these illustrations, it is *devotion that overlooks personal needs and opinions.* It is *focused on people,* and not what we get out of the relationship. And finally, loyalty *endures the failure and shortcomings of people* to whom it's directed.

True disciples are a counter culture, entirely different from the world around us. But, are we? Jesus has always required His followers to go one step beyond what can be done in the natural, for example, loving enemies, not just friends (see Matt. 5:44-47). In Proverbs 27:10, we are told not to forsake a friend (which is a common conviction), or a friend of our father (the step beyond). The value of friendship and loyalty is exemplified in this statement, "Any friend of yours is a friend of mine," a somewhat simple view of loyalty.

Loyalty has gone the way of respect. Personal benefit has become the guiding light as to when to utilize those virtues. This, however, is not true character. Character is consistent regardless of circumstances or personalities. Ultimately, character always has gain, but is never motivated by it. When respect for people fades, so does loyalty.

We live at a time when cults are increasing almost daily. They demand the total allegiance of their disciples. The requirements of discipleship are often manipulative steps to give the leader control over their followers' lives. Is it possible that part of the social "soil" that this aberrant behavior grows out of exists only because of the failure of the church to display the living example of true loyalty? Is it possible that people join these groups because of an instinctive need to be loyal to someone, no matter how humiliating?

In Gideon's day the soldier's cry was, *"For the Lord, and for Gideon!"* (Judg. 7:20). In Joshua's day it was the same. Loyalty to God is seen in our practical devotion to one another—to defend, support, and serve. There is no other way. One could even say that when you've been loyal "to the least of these" you've been loyal to God Himself.

RELEASING YOUR CHILDREN TO GOD

What would you want to get from your house if it were on fire? The most common response is *the pictures.* That is certainly my feeling; rescue the irreplaceable memories. What did people do before Kodak? Grab the drawings and family carvings? How blessed we are!

I've been very emotional in viewing the pictures of my children of late. The memories are priceless. The birthdays, holidays, vacations, first days of school, graduations, and just-plain-cute-children-days all push with vigor my sentimental buttons. Sometimes it's just because they are fond memories, and sometimes it's because those days are finished, and my investment for that part of their lives is over forever.

I've questioned my tears, honestly not understanding them. Sure, there is the feeling that I could have done better as a father. I could have done much better! But at the same time, I have been faithful to my family and to God. They have always been placed *above my ministry.* A perfect father? No. Faithful? Yes. But why the tears?

I'm well into my forties now. I have recently discovered that age can be blamed for just about anything. Perhaps weeping at pictures is a typical response for men my age (though most would never admit it). Maybe it is another evidence that mid-life crises are real—although as yet, I still think they were made up by people who needed another excuse for sin. At 40-something, more than half of life is over for most. But is that the reason for my tears? I don't think so.

Last night something happened that helped me understand a little of what has been going on inside of me. I receive a sad phone call. One of my kids was facing something that hurt deeper than anything he had ever faced before. We shared the pain as a family. There were many tears. And unlike the tears of earlier years, a kiss on their "owie" would not make it better. (I once made the mistake of kissing my little Eric's finger thinking he had an owie, only to discover that I had misunderstood him. In the millisecond that followed that kiss I realized that he had just picked his nose and was only trying to show me.)

A new day requires a new response. On that long-distance call there were many tears, much listening, and carefully selected words of encouragement, followed by much prayer. That night my sleep came with resistance. Grief greeted me as I awoke, and I greeted it with more prayer.

In this crisis I realized something that I should have understood a long time ago. My role has changed. It's not that I didn't know that. I've probably even taught it to others. I just didn't understand it like I do today. There was a time when my daily highlight was to walk through the front door after work and hear Beni say, "Daddy's home." The greatest musical score could never match the beauty of the sound of excited squeals and running feet as my children came to greet me. Nothing will ever replace those magic moments. It is also true that I'll never again be what I was to them then. And that's OK too.

One of my boys was sick and sent home from grade school. Because Beni and I were out of town for the day, they sent him to one of the homes in our church family. He told the grandmother of that household, "I wish my dad was here, because he would pray for me and I would get better." At that age, Mom and Dad are the focus of all solutions. As they grow in the Christian home, their attention is transferred from *Dad having all the answers* to *God having all the answers.* We go from being their source of everything to becoming an advisor and contributor. Soon they pray for their own healing. And when necessary, we join with them in agreement.

The more we succeed in raising responsible children, the less we are needed for the affairs of their everyday life. Our success, in a sense, brings the pain of not being needed the way we were in those early days.

Would I go back? Never! As much as I treasure their season of childhood, I would never go back. Not because of the inherent problems of parenting. Not because of having to relive difficulties. But strangely, because of last night—the brokenness, the transparency, the compassion and consolation, the prayers of intercession, the words of Scripture that were exchanged, were all at a deeper dimension than could ever take place with a small child. It was real life, with both pain and promise.

Parents of young children—it doesn't get easier. But it does get better! Also, it is sometimes a sad reality—*our children are ours on loan.* We have them only for a brief time, a season. Our input is important. But our example is even more so. Teach them through word and example. Cover them daily with prayer. Learn to have fun! And finally, give them back to God. Release them to His will. For in His will there is perfect care.

PASTORS OF WEAVERVILLE

A very unusual thing has happened to our community, something that is rare, and I think encouraging.

I recently met with several pastors in our monthly minister's meeting. We had the privilege of introducing ourselves to the new pastors from both the Lutheran and First Baptist Churches (two very wonderful men). In the introduction we were to mention how long we had been here in Weaverville. I, by the way, was introduced as the *grandfather* of the group.

As we made our proper introductions, I was startled by one consistent factor: each had been in Weaverville for many years. Pastor Tennyson mentioned that he had been here for ten years. Pastor Miller also spoke of her ten years. Father Lawrence mentioned his eleven, and Pastor Ferris his seven. When I mentioned my sixteen years, it became apparent why I was *grandpa*. All these numbers may mean little to you, unless you already see how unusual they are.

Do you have any idea how long a pastor usually stays in a church? The national average is somewhere around two to three years. I'm sure most every city has a pastor or two who have been there for five-plus years, but to have over 50 percent with ten years or more? It's unheard of. And when you add the nearly nonexistent fact that two associate pastors (Bob and Casey) have been here nearly ten years, it's worth taking *special* note.

This city is one with many blessings and benefits. It is also one with many problems. Trinity County is known as a place of poverty. Wages are low, and the esteem of many is even lower. Economically speaking, when the Bay Area sneezes, Redding catches cold and we get pneumonia.

Many jobs and projects are done second-class at best. Many workers have the attitude that doing the minimum is the only way. This area is known for not completing what was started—incomplete shopping centers, industrial parks, etc.

Rumors of the mill closing down are almost a monthly occurrence. Expectations from many of our citizens are depressing. Thankfully, there are exceptions to every example I've given.

Yet God made this city as a jewel, set in majestic forests, cradled by mountains, blessed with four seasons, given the wealth and beauty of abundant natural resources. His plan is good. His promises are perfect; they bring honor to Him and fulfillment to His people.

It's not important who has stayed here and who has left. It matters little how successful any of us have been. What matters is this: circumstances say we are poor and unstable, but God is using the lives of a few of His servants to say something else—stability! Why else would He take so many of His servants and require them to settle down and pour out their lives to a city for so many years? It's His commitment to us all.

Several years ago four pastors all bought their first homes within a few months of each other. Coincidence? I don't think so; the interest rates were not down yet! God wants us to realize that He is building a strong foundation for a significant work. And He is committed to us for the long haul. If pastors change every two to three years, does that mean that God is less committed to that particular community? No. But when He restricts His servants from considering opportunities that come from other places, it is usually proof that the saints have prayed for Him to do a significant work in their city. And that restriction is the beginning of a long-term answer.

Right now, God could move everyone I've listed and still continue His purpose for Weaverville. His plan is not dependent on certain people. Yet it is good to see commitment and stability from the pastorate, when all around the country there are stories of failure, restlessness, and strife.

Mountain Chapel, count your blessings! No, not just Bob and me; it's the pastors of this city. You've honored us many times in many ways. Don't forget to honor these pastors from other churches. They are *elders giving oversight to the church of Weaverville.* And most of all, honor and thank our heavenly Father who has said, "Weaverville, you're special in My sight. I have heard your prayers, and I will do a good work in you, a significant work."

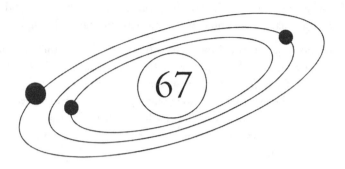

SPIRITUAL ROOTS

Sentiment is a hard thing to define, and even harder to really understand. Emotions and memories are just that way. Sometimes a simple song will release a whole barrage of feelings and thoughts that have their roots in another place and time. The trigger of sentiment can be pulled by a specific date on the calendar, or even by a possession of unusual significance such as, "I bought this camera the day after our first child was born."

This past week I had two unexpected encounters with that friend named sentiment. The first came as I sat in the dedication service for Bethel Church's new building. I was moved deeply, both by the great anointing on the service and the beauty and size of their new facility. But mostly I think God was using my 25 years of memories to stir up the affection of Christ in me for this body of believers that now carries the torch for the house that will forever be the place of my spiritual roots; it was there that I was nurtured and raised up in the faith—it is where I met and married my wife, was released in public ministry, and began raising our family with the birth of our first two children. From there I was sent out to pastor in Weaverville. Bethel is where my spiritual roots are. Bethel is also Mountain Chapel's Mother Church.

The plans for their new building were first drawn when I was there as an associate pastor under my dad, probably about 15 years ago. The original plan included a completely different piece of property. It is good to see people who are willing to pursue and wait, both at the same time. Under the leadership of their pastor Ray Larson they have done the impossible—started the development of their 60-plus acres as a worldwide ministry center—a fitting description for a body that has the world in its sights.

The joy of attending this service was similar to being in a maternity ward as the news of the birth is first pronounced to the anxious family members and friends. It was wonderful, just for what the evening held. But the promise, the anticipation, and the sense of destiny all worked to make the evening one I will remember for a lifetime.

What is it about our spiritual roots that stir up such emotion? Paul, in talking to a group of his converts, said, *"For if you were to have countless tutors in Christ, yet you would not have many fathers, for in Christ Jesus I became your father through the gospel"* (I Cor. 4:15 NASB). This reference was to the fact that there were many people who had played a part in their spiritual growth, but only one was given the privilege of bringing them into the Kingdom. Paul was part of their root system. They were under obligation to him—obligation is the term God uses when we fail to do what is right because of love.

The setting of the second encounter was very different from the first; it was the Christmas service at the jail. Several of the inmates and deputies put on a Christmas program, which in itself was no small miracle. There was wonderful music by very gifted young men and women. They also performed great skits and comedy. Again I was moved. Before my eyes were young men and women who were paying their obligation to society for breaking the law. Yet God used this unplanned detour in their lives as the road to salvation. Our God is just that way.

In this room were the spiritual fathers and mothers of the new believers—Buck, Annie, Dan Hale, and the team. They had planted and watered. God brought about the increase. And these inmates were having etched into their minds the value and uniqueness of their spiritual roots—a little jail in Trinity County.

From the wonderful new facilities of Bethel Church to the humble, manger-like qualities of the Trinity County Jail, God is building people. And you are part of it all. Take delight in the things that matter. Give someone a heritage in Christ with the greatest gift you can give—yourself.

I need to mention that while attending Bethel's dedication service, I sat with the realization that *"the testimony of Jesus is the spirit of prophecy"* (Rev. 19:10 NASB). It was as though God was saying to me, "I first had to bring your spiritual mother into the promise (new facilities). You're next!" Their testimony of provision has become the prophecy of God's promise for us. Our time has come. And just think, what we are about to build will be the spiritual home of thousands, and you will be the mothers and fathers who leave a heritage that will forever mark this generation as one created "for such a time as this."

MOTHERS

I sit waiting. Two and a half hours of my three-hour layover is behind me. The San Francisco International Airport has to be one of the more interesting places to be if you're a people watcher. My wife would be ecstatic (if you look in the dictionary under *people watcher* you should find her picture).

A few feet away is a woman with a baby. The child is about five months old. In watching her I am reminded of the fact that mothers are amazing. There seems to be nothing else that matters besides the child. Her conversation is much like the one she would have with an adult, except for the pitch and the occasional goofy word. She discusses things with the infant that a 10-year-old wouldn't grasp. It matters not. It's her world, and I'm the intruder.

In a way her world seems more real than my own. Mine has a laptop computer begging for entries, a CD player and headphones wishing for an opportunity to entertain, and more books and magazines than could ever be read by me in one trip, all trying to fill in the blanks of the waiting game. The mother's joy is not in techno-toys, it is in life. For most of us waiting or on the plane, our gadgets are to provide the excuse to work and play so that we might not have to interact with strangers.

Women who might normally be concerned about their attire seem to put fashion on the back burner when the baby comes. Let me illustrate. Recently, following a Sunday morning service, I walked up to a young mother and put my hand on her shoulder. I wish I wouldn't have. It was covered with slime—baby slime. And in a very pastoral way I removed my hand without ever revealing my shock or my overall squeamishness over slime of any kind. For mothers of small children, a dry shoulder is unusual. They might have on a beautiful dress, but the shoulders are usually either wet or crusty. And they don't seem to care. Why? A life did it—a very special life.

Mothers do what I consider to be *strange things*. Why would a mother stick her hand down a baby's diaper when they want to see if the child is *completely* through with his or her meal? You can't win by doing that! I realize that touch is one of the senses that God has given us, but my nose works fine. And if for some reason the mess is not detected by my nose, my eyes work really well. Forgive my generalizing, but I've never seen a dad use the *human dipstick method* of checking the diaper. Only mothers. Why the differences between a mom and a dad? I have a theory. Something became stressed during pregnancy that snapped during labor.

The delicate young lady who pouted over a scuffmark on her new pumps is taken through the trauma of carrying the life and weight of another human being around for nine months—each month gaining in intensity and difficulty. After having every possible emotion rage through her heart in a nine-month period, plus the shock of seemingly impossible physiological changes, she is thrust onto the front lines of a war—and she is the general. The one who was once depressed over a broken fingernail now has a grip on her Lamaze-trained husband's arm that frightens him into total submission. After riding the roller coaster of emotions, from the joy of the announced pregnancy to the gut-wrenching labor and delivery, what else is there? They've conquered the planet. It's almost as though the woman does the diaper test to taunt the wimpiness of men, so as to say, *nothing fazes me anymore.*

More than once the apostle Paul referred to maturity in Christ as synonymous with parenting. In First Thessalonians 2:7 he refers to his own ministry as being similar to a nursing mother. He also referred to his own prayer life as one of *labor*, as in giving birth. Maturity in Christ is not always seen in orderliness. The cemetery is the most orderly place in town. Perfect order is sometimes the evidence of death. Maturity is seen in the willingness to live in the private world of the child, one who requires the sacrifice to make nurturing possible, and the determination to do the necessary upkeep—for all relationships require maintenance.

One of my favorite Proverbs is 14:4; it says that a barn without oxen stays clean, but there is an increase that comes because of the oxen (through productivity). People often avoid people. In the church we have our *spiritual* laptops and CDs to protect us from too much interaction. Is it possible that for many their barns are clean and tidy, but they are being robbed of the tremendous blessing of interaction with people? I believe so. If this verse from Proverbs can apply to relationships, what is the implied cost? If we choose the less tidy route, the one filled with people, the barn will need regular cleaning. By nature we bless one another with love, support, and friendship. That's the benefit. But we also bring snotty, drooly shoulders into the equation. Keeping the mess off my *offense list* is the cost. If you want the blessing, get out the shovel and the Handi-wipes.

Mothers, I respect, nay, I fear you! But please don't be offended if I look at your shoulders before touching you. I still have this thing about slime. But don't worry, it's on my *avoid list*, not my *offense list*.

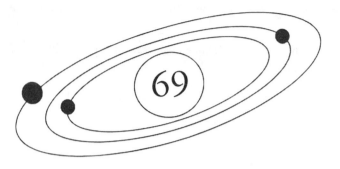

HEROES

Heroes—ordinary people who risk all to save a life. Just as great leadership rises out of crises, so heroes take center stage in the light of tragedy—center stage in the hearts of others, but never at their own request. Being a hero was never planned. It's a heart response. God put it within our nature to give and preserve life. To do anything else is to violate His created order. The hero, even if only for the moment of risk, sees another person's life as more important than his or her own. The Bay Area has been given the privilege of seeing firsthand the greatness of God through the lives of people. I too have enjoyed the stories of common laborers and professionals taking extraordinary risks at the slight chance of saving a life.

My thoughts go back to a couple of years ago when little Jessica fell into a well in Texas. Heroes, all willing to give their lives to save a child, rose to the occasion. Today they fight over the rights to sell the story to Hollywood. Even in San Francisco there are reports of vendors selling bottles of water to those in need for as much as $6 each. It's called supply and demand—good business. Yet there is a higher law. Compassion. Such extremes are easy to spot in a tragedy of this magnitude. No doubt the business that practices *highway robbery* will go belly up once the crisis is over.

But what about everyday life? Are there any heroes? Yes. But they are very few in number. The center stage is removed because there are no crises. Or are there? Those we deem to be heroes think there is. And they are moved by the same passion to preserve life at any cost. They just see things differently. They look at the inevitable destruction coming to a nation, and give themselves to prevent it or at least lessen the devastation. They see the innocent unborn and refuse to call a child a fetus to lessen the guilt of murder. They see the needs of godless neighbors and speak to those less fortunate, and even give out of need. When the true crisis that is all around us is seen, the place of the hero becomes obvious.

The Christian life is such a life. The qualification is giving, like our Father, who *"so loved the world that He gave..."* (see John 3:16).

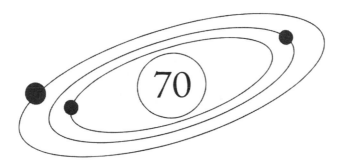

RECEIVING CHRIST'S GIFT

It wasn't too long ago that we sat with our families around the Christmas tree, exchanging gifts in honor of the birth of Jesus. Relatives gathered, some from great distances, to share the joy.

There is something special about the giving of a gift. Sometimes we're simply an observer watching a total stranger open a gift in a restaurant, still moved with joy.

Today we receive a gift. Jesus made and delivers this one to us. He said that He *"gave...prophets"* (Eph. 4:11). Dick Joyce has been that to us for the past 11 years. Time and time again he has come, bringing the word that we need the most, the word that gives us strength and courage. Even those who are new to this body have been affected by his ministry because what we are is due in part to his service to us. Only eternity will disclose the magnitude of his impact.

"Let him who is taught the word share all good things with him who teaches," (Gal. 6:6). We have the privilege of "sharing good things" with this one who has come again to teach us. Whether it's prayer support, the word of encouragement, or a financial gift, it is our joy to give honor where honor is due. *"...appreciate those who diligently labor among you...esteem them very highly in love because of their work"* (1 Thess. 5:12-13 NASB). The way we appreciate the gifts that God has put in our lives is a practical way to demonstrate thankfulness for our salvation.

There has never been a time when I have felt that we failed at this point. Yet as I look to this three-day event, I look with great anticipation and thankfulness. Along with me, let the appreciation in your heart be seen in a practical way. But by far the greatest response is first to receive the word imparted. So let's receive a gift.

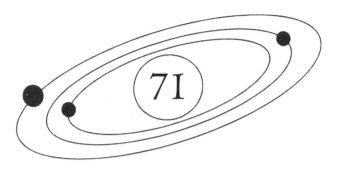

GOOD-BYE TO GRANDMA

Last Saturday Beni and I went to a hospital in Eureka to visit her grandmother. We were called early that morning with the news that she was dying. The kids were quickly taken to various homes for the day. And off we went.

When we arrived, she was not conscious. Perhaps it would be better to say that she could not communicate with us. Often it has been discovered that the one who was thought to be unconscious was very much aware, understanding every word. They just couldn't respond.

We stood next to her bed and told her we loved her. I took that opportunity to thank her for being so good to our kids. Whenever we made the trip to Hoopa for a visit, our kids had quite an adventure. Their home seemed like the place where all the pack rats go to die.

While I hate sickness, I'm thankful that it gave us the opportunity to say things that perhaps should have been said long before. We stayed as long as we could, and said our final good-bye. She died the next morning.

Grandma was a casualty—a victim of extreme legalism, and harmful words of others. She was at one time married to a minister. And as a pastor's wife, she met with much heartache. For reasons unnecessary to mention here, she left her faith. For years the Lord has been drawing her back. Her "restoration" was complete last May. She was in the same hospital, dying, and in extreme pain. In that pain, she had a vision of "the Way, the Truth, and the Life." And in an instant, all pain was gone. Something happened in that divine moment that will be known only in eternity. God put the seal on her life. She belonged to Him. And it's all because we serve a God whose mercy is greater than we could ever comprehend.

Today she is home. And in our tomorrows, we'll be there too.

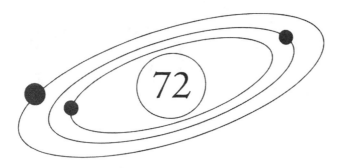

LETTERS FROM KIDS

Apparently the assignment this past week for our Bible Alive children was to "write a note to Pastor Bill." On my desk is a stack of pictures and notes that are cute. Life through the eyes of a child is always refreshing.

Here are some of them, spelling and all:

"Dear Pastor Bill, I am new hear. I don't know you. Bill told me youer name. Sensearly, Davy."

"Dear Pastor Bill, do you like my pictur? Jessica."

"Dere Pastor Bill, thank you for making childrens sundy school papers...when I grow up I would like to sing on the stag with you. I love you Bill. Danielle."

"Dear Pastor Bill, I like lisening to you at church. And sometimes at homgroup. Love, Miriah."

"Dear Pastor Bill, I've only missed church two times. Love, Jacob. P.S. I like your tie."

"Dear Pastor Bill, you'r tie sometimes it's wild. Sometimes it's silly and sometimes it's COOL. you'r a good pastor. from Stephanie."

"Dear Pastor Bill, one thing I like about you is you have good taste in sweets. Jesse. P.S. I like your wild ties."

While I didn't include them all here, the ties won over my sermons about 2 to 1. But the two notes that I didn't like addressed me as, "Dear Past Bill." What do they know that I don't?

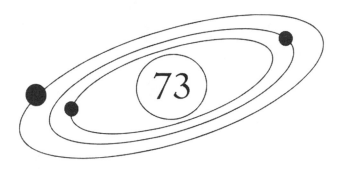

RECEIVING DICK JOYCE

I believe it was November when I received a phone call from Dick Joyce saying that he was available to come to Weaverville in January. He was scheduled to come in May of this year, but because of a cancellation, he was able to move up the meetings to this month. Something in my heart leaped in witness to God's timing for us. Indeed, this was God's timing.

Dick is a gift to this body. He carries a concern for us through the many months of the year that he is not in Trinity County. We talk often by phone to discuss the condition of the church at large, and specifically you and me. He brings a word to us that is always timely. The word is a word of power. And with the word is an experience for those who are hungry. Some churches offer good education in the knowledge of the Scriptures. Others offer an experience. I want us to have both in good measure. It is in the combination of "knowing" and "doing" that the gospel is displayed in power.

Many thanks to you for your prayers and participation in this series of meetings. It made me feel really proud to be your pastor. Your generous financial support enabled us to send Dick away with a good love gift to help make up for "recession's bite." But most of all, thanks for receiving the word that was given. All the other notes of commendation are worth little to me without this final one. We listened, received, and responded to the word of the Lord. My one word of encouragement to each of you is to take some time to consider what the Lord spoke into your life and how you can better give place to that new work. Remember, "The winter is past!" Hallelujah!

Our foster children who lost their mother to suicide a little over a year ago found out this past week that their father died last Thursday. Many of you have been praying for them. Thanks! They are doing well.

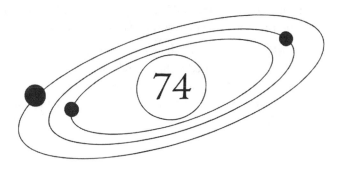

STUDENTS

Twenty years ago Beni and I attended Genesis Discipleship Training Center in Santa Rosa. Annually, I make the trek to teach at that fine Bible school for a week. It's always a highlight in my year.

When I travel overseas, some of my favorite ministry time is also in Bible schools. What is it about a student that is so appealing to a Bible teacher? It's fun to feed hungry people.

Sometimes when I teach in pastors' conferences, which I love to do, it takes a session or two to obtain the necessary favor from them. When I do, it's great fun.

Many pastors suffer a lot of mental and emotional abuse, and often come to these conferences suspicious and/or defensive. It often takes a little time for them to sense another pastor's heart and be able to receive from him. When I have their favor, there's no greater joy in ministry.

Students are the most interesting group, though. They ask questions about things that the previous generation never thought of. The idea of tolerating anything less than ideal is foreign to them—by nature they are driven to change. Usually when they are convinced that something is right, no one can get them to budge from their position—"It's a matter of principle." I love students. I always have.

I like to go to the kind of places that students go to—their bookstores, coffee shops (espresso bars), beaches, and stores. I prefer some of their clothes, their music styles, and especially their sense of adventure. Yet I'm realizing that I must be careful. I'm getting to the age where all this will be attributed to me having a mid-life crisis. Forgive me if that is one of your sacred cows, but I don't believe there is such a crisis. However, if I ever walk around with my shirt open down to my navel, and wear a big gold chain around my neck with a pendant on it bearing the name of Elvis, please buy me a book on the subject.

Since the word *disciple* means "learner," all who follow Christ are students. Maybe part of the childlike faith that we are required to have can be found in the life of a student— eager to learn, adventurous, idealistic, and committed to change wherever it's needed. Perhaps that's why this church has always been my favorite "student body." It's good to be home.

My Children

I'm torn inside. Both joy and sorrow are at war in me, trying to lay claim to the same thing: my children. My joy is for them—seeing them grow and becoming responsible individuals. Their lives are unfolding in a glorious way. It's exciting to see God's hand upon them and their response to His work. That alone is worth life itself.

As mentioned previously, my sorrow is for me. I don't get another chance.

I entered parenthood as most do—excited and fearful. It didn't take long for me to realize my inadequacy. Yet my ideals remain intact, in spite of me. My family has the top priority of my heart, even above my ministry. Only Jesus receives more of me.

As all parents do, I've cried, been afraid, regretted bad decisions, and perhaps laughed more than my share. The tear in my heart is growing, and out of it comes an increasing flow of joy and sorrow. As far as I can tell, it's an unavoidable wound. My kids are getting older and I can see the day approaching when they will leave the nest to build one for themselves.

I hear that being a grandparent is great. It is also apparent that there is joy in seeing your children become contributors to society, standing on their own. But honestly, I have found very little comfort in all of that.

Did I do a good job? They're doing well. I'm so proud of them. But did I do my best? Was Christ represented to the best of my abilities in my home? You see, I don't get another chance.

These are the questions that I've been asking myself. I've found rest only in the truth that "love covers a multitude of sins." On my best day it's only His grace that makes my efforts effective. And on my worst, it's His grace again that covers my obvious lack. Lest

I sound too introspective, let me say that these questions have made me more determined to make the most of today. I don't want anything wasted. Time, life's greatest commodity, is in short supply.

And so, today I will embrace my children again. I'll tell them with my words and actions how much they mean to me. I will work to nourish them on the tender balance of discipline and adventure, of work and play. And again, I am willing to pay the price to build the memories that will serve as beacons of light for any dark day that might lie ahead.

Until now, I've quietly kept this sorrow mostly to myself. Who knows, maybe in some small way I'll be able to better understand what it was like for the Father to give His only Son. I'm broken because of my pending loss. I can't begin to comprehend His. But I do give thanks. And to the Father I offer my best—I offer my children.

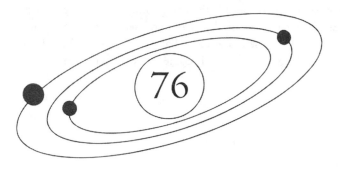

FRIENDS

This morning I caught myself daydreaming, thinking of some of my greatest friends. Interestingly enough, not all of them do I know really well or have I known for a long time. Why then would I call them my greatest friends? Because quality has power over quantity.

Dick Mills wrote me a letter this past week. It's something that he does quite often. He serves everyone with encouragement. If Beni and I see him at a conference, we become his guests of honor. He'll give us much of his precious time, always building us up, never with a negative word. Thankfully, he's not above correcting me if he feels I need it. (The Bible says that, *"he who hates correction is stupid"* [Prov. 12:1] Ouch!) Oh, don't get me wrong. He doesn't look for things to pick on. He just helps me to be conformed by the Word. He's a friend—faithfully so.

Dick Joyce is one I speak to frequently by phone discussing Weaverville, his travels, or what God is saying to the church. In January I travel with him to India to speak in a pastors' conference. He spends time with me, giving me guidance and counsel. Our families try to have one vacation-type activity together every summer. It's been fun. And he is my friend—faithfully so.

Time doesn't afford me the privilege to speak of Iverna or my dad. Neither does it allow me to brag on Bob or Buck or any of the other great men in the church. Yet each of these has a continual impact on my life because of their giving. You, the ones who know me best (and my worst) are friends. And my life is forever shaped by your love. Thanks!

But why do so many suffer when it comes to friendships? One answer is rather simple. It's found in John 12:24, *"Unless a grain of wheat falls into the earth and dies, it remains alone."* Notice the risk involved here. The fear to give of oneself sacrificially—die—causes us to remain *alone*. It's almost as if attempting to have a new friend is the very thing that disqualifies us. But being friendly by giving and self-sacrificing is the basis for all true friendship. To grasp for myself is to lose what is mine. Remember, the laws of this Kingdom are different. We give to receive, become the least to become great, and die to live.

PRAYER IN THE MARKETPLACE

The look in the waitress's eyes was that of "controlled shock." She had just asked me to pray for her—meaning sometime during the day remember her in prayer. Of course I said yes. Not wanting to embarrass her, I looked to see if there was anyone else in the restaurant. There wasn't, so I asked if I could pray for her now. The look of surprise was over the "now" part. She paused for quite awhile, perhaps hoping I would tell her that I was just kidding. I grabbed her hand and prayed.

There are many religions. There are many spirits and powers. But there is only one God, One Truth. That was my opportunity to introduce her to the reality of God's presence through prayer. It's my conviction that we owe that to this world—an experience with God.

A businessman tells me of the arthritis that is about to force his early retirement. It was a cry for help, one that I couldn't answer. But Jesus could. A simple prayer in the "marketplace" gave Jesus a chance to meet him at his place of need. To this day, many years later, the arthritis is gone.

A retired man is suffering with asthma. His confession of need gives me an opportunity to "give him Jesus."

God hungers for the chance to encourage and bless people. Remember, He's not walking out of the halls of Heaven looking for a chance to wipe us all out. For Him that would be rather simple. He is looking for the open door to provide His solutions for our problems. And here's the wonderful truth—we open that door through prayer.

As people come to you with the problems of life, give them Jesus. Let them experience the power of God's presence through your presence.

Here are a few simple guidelines:

1. Live with an awareness of God's presence. You'll be more inclined to be used in that way if your own communion with Him is intact.

2. Don't pray in a manner that draws attention away from God.

3. Be careful not to pray in an environment that would bring them embarrassment. Protect their dignity.

4. Don't preach in your prayer. Don't pretend to say something to God that was really intended for the person you are praying for.

5. Resist the temptation to give counsel. First give God an opportunity to make His heart known to them intimately.

6. Finally, be sincere, and keep it simple. There are no prizes given for grandiose prayers.

God has equipped us for ministry to the lost. We are one of God's "Lost and Found." And if we are ready to serve them with prayer, they'll trust us with their problems.

Servants: Arise, go, and pray!

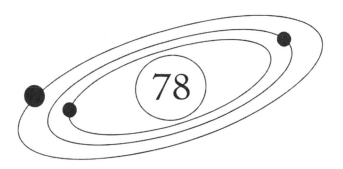

Good News

Several years ago, a friend of mine, along with a number of other Christian businessmen, took a shipload of building supplies to Nicaragua to help the poor. They built homes from those materials and gave them to the people. A short time later they saw these same houses on the network news with a correspondent reporting how good the Communists were to the poor to build these homes for them.

During the reign of President Carter there was a gathering for Christians in Washington, DC. There were an estimated 600,000 people gathered for the event, just to pray for this nation. All the networks were notified. Not one was willing to report on the event. Even President Carter, a professing Christian, refused to acknowledge it. Yet if there are a couple thousand homosexuals or even a half a dozen wanting a sex change, the networks are there. Am I bitter? No. Quite frankly, we don't need the world promoting the church. The one time a demon-possessed girl promoted Paul's ministry by saying he was a man of God and spoke the truth (all true statements), he rebuked her and cast out the demon. I'm just mystified. Bob Dylan wrote, "There is none so blind as them that will not see." Bad news is in vogue, and it has been for quite some time, even among Christians.

Back in the '70s, Logos Publishers tried to create a newspaper that only had good news. But it didn't sell. And Logos went bankrupt over the endeavor. Good news doesn't sell. The hunger of our nation is for the bizarre. The weirder the better. Just look at the daytime talk shows. (Better yet, *don't* look at the daytime talk shows.)

When President Reagan was shot, the news traveled around the world in moments. People on the streets were talking about it, and every television station carried the story. Jesus wasn't only wounded, He died in our place. And it still hasn't gotten around the world, after 2,000 years. But still, it is good news. It's the best news. Share it; the networks never will.

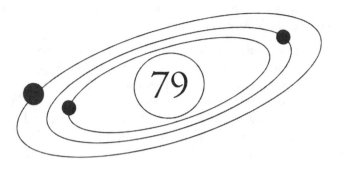

MARKETING SCHEMES

You'd think that a billion dollar industry like dentistry could come up with a better name for a procedure than *root canal*. It was probably named by the same guy who thought of *spinal tap*. I guess they figure if you're in great pain you don't care what they call it. But I think they could use a good Public Relations person.

We live in fun times. Oh, I know they are difficult; perhaps *perilous* would be a better term. But I still think they are fun. For example: last week we watched the Super Bowl with about eight to ten other loud people. We'd root and yell, and stand up with our hands in the air when our team did something good—which wasn't often enough. But when the commercials came on, everyone was silent. Why? The Super Bowl has the best ads of the year. Marketing genius is seen during this annual event—as well as further proof that alcohol destroys brain cells, i.e., The Bud Bowl?

One year I was in India during this game. My family recorded it for me so that I could watch it when I got home. Since the 49ers weren't playing I just fast-forwarded to the commercials. It was great.

Can you imagine what it would be like if the dental industry had the same marketing people working for them who represent companies like Nike or Burger King? The root canal would be called "tooth renewal, from the inside." For those who need their information in a cruder fashion they could call the drill "The Exorcist." Somehow, the marketing agent, similar to the politician, is able to candy-coat the bad news in such a way that you're almost thankful you have it so hard.

My favorite fly-fishing magazine used to be published seven times a year. I'll never forget when I received their letter telling me they were reducing it to six. Someone in their

PR department wrote it in such a way that I was almost happy I would receive this fine periodical less often. That's marketing genius.

Some would like to see the church use the Madison Avenue approach to reaching the lost. After all, with them on our side, we could present the Good News in such a way so as not to offend anyone. (If only John the Baptist had been born in a time more appropriate for his need.) We could replace "Repent, you brood of vipers" with "Make a turn for the better, you friend of all animals." Instead of Judgment Day, we'd call it "The Forever Sweepstakes!" And that ugly word "sin" could be called "human rights." And of course, to please everyone, it would no longer do to have a "heavenly Father." It would now have to be "heavenly Person."

As dumb as they sound, many have come close to such attempts at being culturally current. Being understood is important, but relevance is not a product of human reasoning. No one is more *now* than God; He is the great I Am! No one understands humanity better than our Creator. He has never offered an updated version of His Word. It was given as the gift that would span all time, sufficient for every human need, containing both the wisdom and power to transform human nature, which isn't inherently good! While it may not be politically or even religiously correct, *"All have sinned and fall short of the glory of God"* (Rom. 3:23), remains the truth.

Go ahead, be entertained by how many ways they can try to sell you a can of soda. But give the gospel its purest form, word for Word, His way.

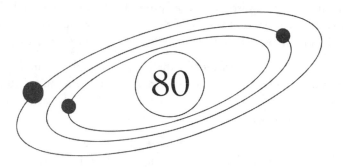

RAIN

A musical cadence has been set by constant dripping from my leaky office ceiling. The buckets, bowls, and jars are in place. My desk chair is drying off in front of the heater. And a plastic tarp is semi-neatly hidden from view. It covered my desk during the night to protect it from further water damage. I think I might even have enough water collecting in the corner to stock a few bass.

Rain is good. It replenishes the earth and helps things to grow. It provides snow for our mountains, and water for our lakes. But don't forget, it's also messy; especially if there is a lot of it all at once. It will uproot the biggest tree. In fact, it will move a mountain if the conditions are right. This week I saw a million-dollar home completely destroyed by rain. It simply fell into a hole created by the storm. And I have to remind myself, as I sit in my new little rain forest, rain doesn't create leaks; it discovers them.

People's opinion of rain changes with the seasons. During the hot, dry times, most everyone would like a nice shower or two to help cool things off. But a summer shower can also bring lightning and subsequent fires. And it's often the spring rains, with the accompanying snow runoff, that cause flooding. Rain is just unpredictable.

The most frustrating thing about rain is that we just can't control it. And God knows how much we've tried. The whole concept of damming our rivers is rooted in our attempt to control this heavenly blessing. And then there's "cloud seeding" done via an airplane. It is supposed to help release the water content contained in the cloud. If there were ever a people who thrived on controlling their environment, it would have to be us. Temperature, smell, color, humidity, and sound all attract the American's investment dollar as we attempt to have more control over our surroundings. But the weather is still out of our reach.

Rain is a subject often discussed in Scripture. In the natural it symbolizes blessing and prosperity. In the spiritual it speaks of the work of the Holy Spirit, and sometimes even speaks of God Himself, as in Hosea 6:3, "...*He will come to us like the rain....*"

Our word *revival* is often portrayed by the biblical metaphor, rain. Many of us pray for revival, hoping for a nice spring rain—warm, mild, and refreshing. Most of us, however, don't want a downpour. That brings inconvenience. But then, neither do we want so little that we feel unspiritual.

The rains of revival are as messy as any we've seen on the evening news. They discover leaks in our homes and bring hidden debris out into the open. And in some situations, they have even been known to bring division, much like the house that crashed into a sinkhole. Those who say revival doesn't bring conflict need to reread their Bibles. Both Scripture and church history testify to the sometimes puzzling effect of rain. In great portions, it simply overpowers whatever stands in its way.

Just as great storms don't always allow us to retain control of our environment, so revival challenges our tight grip on the reins of life, painfully exposing our intolerance for not being in control. In history, some of the participants in revival have even turned on each other. I'm reminded of a pastor who was leading his church family into a "normal" service when uncontrollable laughter broke out. Of course the critics blamed the laughter on the pastor, as though he could cause rain by merely speaking about joy. (Once while Moses was dealing with some problem-causing Israelites, the earth opened up and ate them. The survivors blamed Moses.) Perhaps we leaders are given too much credit. I've yet to meet the man who can open up the earth, or make religious people laugh beyond control and receive a true heart change.

The *rain* that I've witnessed in recent days has not only made things less predictable, it's provided the catalyst for great change in all who have embraced what God is doing. Never have I witnessed such dramatic healing of the heart. Never. And you can trace it all back to this thing that works best when it's beyond our control—rain. You'll enjoy it best if you embrace it...but don't stand in its way.

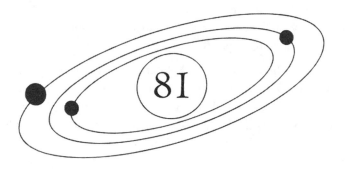

TORONTO

The British Press calls it the *Toronto Blessing*. Dick Joyce also refers to it as the *Jerusalem Blessing*, as that's where it started almost 2,000 years ago. Last March I was able to go and witness the outpouring of this *Blessing* for myself, and at the same time invite God's deeper work in me. The hand of God was quite evident.

Beni and I just returned from a second trip. The phrase, "God sometimes offends our minds to reveal what's in our hearts," makes a lot of sense when you see such unusual demonstrations of God's power. Some of it is quite humorous. And I think being able to laugh at how God has chosen to work in His people can even be healthy.

One evening, near the exit of the Toronto Airport Vineyard Church sanctuary, there was a very anointed man of God walking around looking for people to touch with God's power. This whole section of the building seemed to have an unusual sense of God's presence. I called this area the Bermuda Triangle. You might get out through there, but you'll not be the same as when you entered.

As Beni and I were leaving, having been at church for about six hours that evening, the man looked at her from a distance and saw God at work—like a hawk zooming in on its prey, he walked toward her. I was holding her hand as the power of God hit, which was before he even touched her. And "hit" is a good word for what happened. She began to shake like frog legs in a frying pan. It was almost violent. Yet for her it was a wonderful encounter with God, so peaceful that her whole cry was for more, no matter what!

Some critics have said that all of this is the result of mass hysteria. Others have said it's the work of the devil. Still others have pointed to the whole movement as a demonstration of flesh. But none of those three have a reputation for increasing one's hunger for God, His Word, and a love for His people. The ongoing fruit of those who have been touched by God in this season of renewal is an obvious testimony of the great love of the Father—the only validation needed to distinguish a genuine move of God. We are continually amazed and hunger for little else.

Many who go to Toronto receive such an anointing on their lives that it affects everything they do. Going to a restaurant in Toronto is sometimes interesting. People will shake or laugh uncontrollably simply from praying over their meal. Some will jerk in a way that makes the waitress think they have a disease. I've also seen people come under the power of God by simply being close to someone who began to sing a worship chorus while walking down the hall of a hotel.

Why would God do this? I haven't a clue. But don't complain...there was a time in Scripture when there was no evidence of God for 400 years! And in order to grow in what I've experienced in my own divine encounter, I'll gladly look like a fool for more.

It's fun to see God working in people you know. Especially when you know they are not given to seeking attention or pursuing weird things. My father-in-law is a very quiet and controlled godly man. After God's touch, he looked more like a great warrior who had too much to drink. He is forever ruined—what a way to go. He hungers for nothing else but God.

It's amazing to see God working in one so violently and in another so quietly. Many fall, while others stand with no visible reaction. God is at work in both, and the fruit is the same. I've seen those who have wanted something unusual to happen to them, only to have nothing out of the ordinary take place. And still others who have feared that something unusual would happen to them, actually come under His power in ways that would scare anyone, except the one it happens to. Even the skeptic gets up after such an encounter with God wanting little else out of life than more of God.

The fact that some who display manifestations are making things up to get attention doesn't nullify the real work of God. The fact that some stand in resistance to God working in them as He pleases doesn't nullify the fact that many who stand, showing no outward manifestation of God's presence, have been deeply touched by God.

This is a mysterious season, which is one of the reasons I like it so much. The experts can't give a complete explanation. And the critics can't deny its fruit. To top it off, it's on the verge of being *out of our control*. Inviting, isn't it?

Some pursue God because they hunger for more of His power in their lives. Some hunger for more knowledge and understanding. There are those who want ministry success, and still others who seek Him because they want specific answers to prayer. There are many reasons that have motivated people to seek God in this unique season. But it seems that no matter what the motive is for people to enter this movement, all come out with a greater revelation of the Father's love, simply hungering for more of God.

I've been encouraging people to embrace this renewal. It is God. Having been ruined for life, I'm now encouraging people to simply embrace God...all that you can.

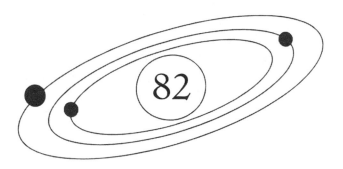

GRADUATION

Congratulations to the graduates! Trinity County Christian School had its graduation this past week. What a thrill it was to see the first class that attended the school from pre-school through the eighth grade. God has used this fine school to establish character and direction in many lives. Thank you to all who have supported this school through the years. It's paying off!

We have a number of youth who graduate this next week from both the eighth grade and high school. The Bible says that *"youth are to you as the dew"* (Ps. 110:3 NASB). Dew is a mark of God's blessing. Youth are a gift to us from God, and as such they are to be treasured. Children and youth remind us of the Kingdom of God. The simplicity of life, sense of adventure, innocence and dreams, all testify of a superior way of life—God's way. It's called the Kingdom of God.

The enemy works hard to destroy children by destroying childhood. When a civilization loses that, they have lost the witness of God's approach to life. Rise up and give your support to these great kids.

David committed a great sin with Bathsheba. To cover his immorality he had her husband killed. The method used was interesting. Joab, the commander of the army, put Uriah on the front lines of battle and withdrew from him. Having no support or protection by himself, he died.

Our missionaries sometimes find themselves in a similar position to Uriah: sent to the frontlines of battle, but being forgotten by the ones who sent them. We have sent them, and many have withdrawn their support. "Out of sight, out of mind," some may say. My response is, "Then where are you looking?" Let's rally behind these men and women of God who, like their Lord, have laid it all down for the cause of the King and His Kingdom. Pray and give.

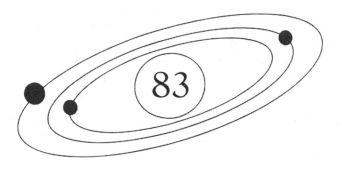

FIND THE NEEDY

The East Coast of the United States is considered by many to be the graveyard of the evangelist. Their resistance to the gospel has existed for many years. It is said that Charles Finney considered it to be the hardest place in which he had ever ministered. But God...

I just returned from a ten-day trip to Massachusetts. The birth of this nation took place in that part of the country. They have great pride in their heritage. It's the land of "Kennedy politics" and much religious tradition. If anyone needed to be convinced of the negative effect of religion, they should look no further. New England is plagued with *form without power.* I guess it could be said, *powerless religion has a power of its own.*

In the midst of such resistance is God at work. He is building His church and the gates of hell will not prevail. Near the New Hampshire border are several churches that are flourishing. The life of Christ reigns supreme as the worshiping community of believers is making its mark. A point that has been made regarding this present revival is that it is not one formed around a particular teaching or doctrine. It is focused on worship. Each time I visit New England I see God raising up a people to make an impact on the Babylon in which they live. Signs and wonders are on the increase. And they all love to worship God.

The last five days of my trip were spent in a community about 30 minutes out of Boston. This group of believers is one of the most unusual you'll find anywhere. When Mario Murillo wrote his book *Fresh Fire,* he spoke of the Lazarus Generation. They are the forgotten, abused, and destroyed. Yet God resurrects them into His army. Their church is a Lazarus group. The rejects of society are there, healed and in their right minds.

Think about it. The world has more and more throwaways—they are the addicts, the homeless, the criminals, the misfits. Because the world has no answer but to drug them and keep them out of harm's way—and out of ours—there is an opportunity for the gospel that even New England will take notice of. It is time for the gospel to be preached with power! And it is being declared by a few who care nothing for themselves, be it reputation or favor or personal gain. They simply declare God's Word and rejoice in the fruit.

This unusual fellowship that I spoke of is comprised of people out of the mafia, the homosexual movement, the homeless, high-powered business people, the sick (including AIDS), and the religious. How moving it is to stand there and see the power of God at work among the people. They are so hungry. And they are so grateful for all that God provides for them. You enabled me to be a blessing to them. Thank you.

All of this brings me to one of the directives that God put in my heart many years ago.

> *"In that day," says the Lord, "I will assemble the lame, I will gather the outcast and those whom I have afflicted; I will make the lame a remnant, and the outcast a strong nation..."* (Micah 4:6-7).

That's us! God is interested in the lame. His heart goes out to those who have no one else to turn to. It is in His heart to bring hope to those rejected by society. In fact, His Kingdom is filled with those who knew they didn't fit in this one.

There is one fact concerning evangelism that has always remained true—go to the needy and people will be saved. Whether it is the wealthy in crisis or the poor in their daily environment, the needy respond to Jesus. Why? Because when we finally come to the end of ourselves, there is room for a miracle. This is why the gospel must be preached with power. It is to be presented to people who are broken and in need. When we minister to these people, we *must* have power. Cute stories and jokes won't rescue them from destruction. Only the gospel. Only Jesus.

I never cease to be amazed at how people's lives are transformed in the preaching of God's Word. The greatest privilege that comes from my relationship with Jesus is to preach. If you haven't done so yet, join me. Find the needy, speak the Word, and pray.

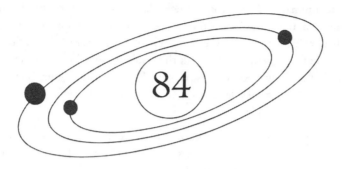

AN ALTERNATIVE, NOT A PROTEST

"Jesus Christ Superstar"! Do you remember it? It was a play and a movie that hit this nation at the tail end of the "Jesus Movement" of the late '60s and early '70s. Their portrayal of Christ was somewhat typical of the secular marketplace; He was what we would call "worldly," from their point of view. It was, however, a statement of the times to have a presentation of Jesus so heavily viewed by the younger generation.

Many of us had gathered at Shasta College to share our faith with those who had come to see the movie. Not all of us were clear about why we were there, as some showed up to protest Jesus being portrayed in that manner. I remember one individual asking a young lady named Debbie if she had seen the movie. She said no, to which they responded, "Why then are you in protest of something you haven't seen?"

You know as I do that the church in recent days has been known for protest much more than what Christ said our ID card was to be...love. Debbie responded by saying that she wasn't protesting anything; she just wanted to share the love of Jesus with anyone who would listen. Not only did she silence her accuser; it taught me a valuable lesson.

Here it is 21 years later, and I still feel what I felt that evening whenever I think of that encounter—an appreciation for having a positive message. Think about it. Our message is not a negative one—although the enemy has succeeded at times in getting us to focus on what we're *against* instead of what we are *for*. Jesus is called God's "Yes" in Second Corinthians 1.

Bob and I had a staff meeting this morning at a local restaurant. A woman present asked Bob for a chapter and verse from the Bible that says we shouldn't allow our kids to participate in school dances. Depending on who we are talking with, this can be a sore subject. Yet the question was one that deserved an answer—especially since there is no verse with that command. (I need you to know that I don't like the school dances. There is nothing about them that would make me feel good about encouraging our kids to go. The music, the physical movement, and the environment are all that of sensuality. I believe it is just another tool of the enemy used to sink the hook of worldliness into the hearts of our Christian youth. But, I must admit, it is possible for a Christian young person to go there and be unscathed by the devil's devices, especially if they go as evangelists. Yet, dancing is not even the focus for this piece.)

Unfortunately, we are sometimes known for what we oppose, be it abortion, school dances, or whatever. It's not a compliment to bear that "tag" in life, especially considering the awesome message we have to offer.

Let's look at this subject as an example of a greater message that we all share, whether or not you agree with my convictions about school dances. I will not lead or try to inspire a movement to rid our school of this event. It is not a noble enough cause to absorb so much of my efforts. I won't even tell our kids that they shouldn't go, in the sense that they will be a "sinning saint" if they do.

My life's message is this: *Know God.* A cop-out? No. In knowing Him, He becomes the reason behind our decisions, and the standard for what is worthwhile. If you or anyone else thinks that our message is anti-anything, it's a sign of our losing perspective on the real commission.

Some may ask, "Is your Dance Alternative a form of protest against the direction that the school is taking?" Definitely not. We provide an alternative because we believe that we can provide more fun at a better price and with less risk of taking on the world's mindset. Protest? No. Better? Absolutely!

Many churches have as their primary message an attack on what is wrong with our world—and in some cases, what is wrong with the church. It may be an emphasis on teaching people how to deal with cults. It might be training on how to change our social ills. It could even be an attack on another part of the church that is different from their theology—such as the issue of speaking in tongues.

Each of those subjects has merit for study. But none of them has the value to become our life's message. That message is determined by our focus; it's either on what is wrong, or on the One who is right.

Our answer to the woman in the restaurant? We don't care for dances because of the sexual and rebellious atmosphere. But we don't condemn anyone for going. If there is a dance and you don't believe there is anything wrong with it, we believe that we can create an activity that not only doesn't have the elements we find questionable, but one that can be more fun and be a *positive* experience too. We provide an alternative, not a protest.

It's obvious; I don't like the dances. But it's not my message. Mine is best summarized by a T-shirt I saw recently: Know God, no hell. No God, know hell!

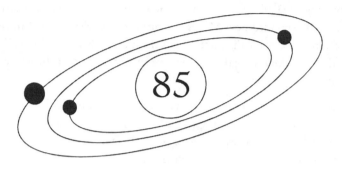

His Gospel

Today was a unique one. I spent the morning opening the Scriptures to a group of young men from *Where Eagles Soar*, a Christ-centered drug rehab center in Redding. It was my privilege to share about one of my favorite passages: *"Rejoice always; pray without ceasing; in everything give thanks..."* (I Thess. 5:16-18). I've often said that if I could learn to live those verses perfectly, I'd have it made—arriving early at sainthood.

Speaking to young Christians is a treat. It reminds me somewhat of a statement my Uncle David makes, "Every household needs a two-year-old." A two-year-old has no regard for possessions, which is seen in how many things they can break in a day. That really messes up our material world. They have little class or social skills, which doesn't help us with our eternal quest to *look good in the eyes of others.* They bring a whole new meaning to *eating out.*

Teaching new Christians helps us with priorities. Plus, their newfound love for God is contagious. Their questions force honesty upon us because they don't adapt well to answers that are just theories. I enjoy searching my own heart for the real stuff. It is truly an honor.

After the drive home, I began to prepare my heart for a meeting that would prove to make this day more than different. The meeting was for people who work with the dying. That is not something that most of us experience in a normal day. Yet that is not what made it different. It was the fact that I was on a panel of six that included a Buddhist, a Catholic priest, a Congregational church pastor, a Native Indian religious leader, and an Eastern Orthodox woman from a monastery.

We were each given a theoretical five minutes to present our approach to death. Following our message, the floor was opened for questions. I was amazed at how other religious groups use the biblical concept of the testimony. Everyone has a story to prove their beliefs. I was reminded how Moses might have felt when after throwing down his rod, it turned into a snake. He then watched as the magicians did the same. They were also able to provide the onlookers with an experience to confirm their beliefs, except Moses' snake ate theirs—minor details!

The Buddhist spoke of some who have died who had reached such a state of consciousness that their bodies just disappeared, going on to their next life. The Native American shared his sweatbox experiences, with the corresponding visions and experiences with eagles used to bring him divine messages.

In the past, I'd always felt that a testimony was the thing to share in that environment. But, I became very much aware of the possibility of trying to "one up" the previous person and chose not to do that. Besides, God has no real competition. Nothing is more powerful than the simple message of the gospel. I shared how death is especially fearful for those who hope that they have been "good enough" to go to Heaven. The believer places their hope in the fact that Jesus was good enough for them, period. Jesus is the message. And I am not ashamed of Him!

I prayed for God to reveal the truth to these people. It is easy to want God to show Himself strong because I want to appear right before everyone else. It's similar to the woman who prays for her husband to be converted because she wants him to say she was right all along. Or the person who wants to be healed because he or she wants the doctor to look bad. Certainly these are not the best of motives. As I prayed, I made sure to pray for the name of Jesus to be honored. It honestly mattered little how I looked to anyone else. And to test whether or not my prayer was genuine, He gave me the *gift of tears,* the one I wanted the least. I wept as I recalled the last experience of working with the dying—my friends who lost both of their teenaged sons. To weep in front of you...no problem. "But God, not in front of *them!*" Oh well.

How did it turn out? I don't know for sure. But I enjoyed it, much the same way Daniel enjoyed entering the lion's den. Fearfully excited, but without a clue as to how it would end for sure. I hope that someone was affected by this wonderful gospel. Yet I'm fairly certain that I was affected more by them than they were by me. Instead of contempt for ideologies that I know are born in the heart of the father of lies, I felt a love for people who I pray will one day embrace the same Savior as I. Many of them are from parts of this community that we have yet to touch.

But tonight I sat praying in the Holy Spirit over people God has promised will someday come to the knowledge of the truth.

It's easy for us Christians to act at times as though this is *our gospel.* Perhaps it would be best for us to think of it in this way. *The story of salvation is not my gospel. It is His. I do not possess the truth. He possesses me!*

If there is anything learned from this experience, it was how many unconverted people operate in their gift. They are simply learning how to use what will one day be useful to bring glory to the King. And I pray earnestly for that day.

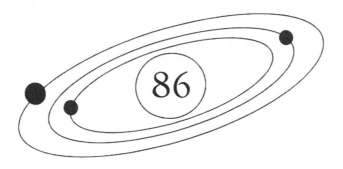

BUILDING THE HOUSE

Put on your seat belts. We are in for a wild ride. God is stirring things up and none of us will be left idle. Each of us will be brought to a place of challenge and change. How do I know this? My own experience.

As you know, we have sold our home out on East Weaver. We are buying a home in town. And this home needs work. Much work. Many of you have learned that I am not the best Jack-of-all-trades. In fact, Jack, I have no trades. For me to work around the house is for me to provide enough material for ten comedians to work full time. (Actually, I have successfully repaired my dryer many times—a sure sign of God's abundant grace.)

This may seem silly to you, but God has cornered me. I have no choice but to learn to work on my house. Today I start tearing out the old deck (escrow cannot close until it is replaced) and build a new one. Then, after escrow closes, we tear out the carpets, scrape the ceilings of their acoustical something-or-other, knock out a wall or two (which Brian Barrow is doing—hallelujah!), and who knows what else. I have searched and searched, and there are no other options.

Forgive me for taking what would be trite and insignificant for many of you and spiritualizing it as a word for the whole church. If this all pertained only to material things, I would probably be silent, except for a joke or two. But in my spirit I am experiencing similar things. I have been placed into a position that is very un-comfortable. Yet to be completely honest, deep inside I'm excited. Excited because we are moving into the unknown with this knowledge—He is with us and will lead us into victory.

Remember, the higher the risk, the greater the miracle. While I don't like to be uncomfortable, I apparently need it. What gives me discomfort with my house is similar to what I feel about God's house—us. I'm excited because He's the builder, and nervous because...I guess I have no reason.

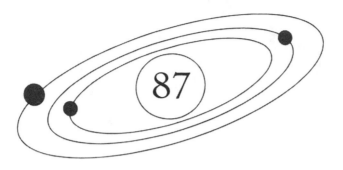

THOUGHTS ON TRAVEL

This past week I taught at Genesis, a Bible training center in Santa Rosa mentioned previously. This is the school that Beni and I attended in 1972-73. It was a tremendous week. God did such a wonderful work in the lives of those hungry students. We ended the week with about one and a half hours of personal ministry. There was a good anointing of the Holy Spirit present. Thanks for your prayer support.

One of the great things about traveling in ministry is that once you get 25 miles from home you're considered an expert. I may not know anything, but they don't know that. But then, of course, God has a way of bursting that short-lived bubble. Real life has a way of bringing all of us to our real level of faith.

A friend of mine, who travels in ministry, shared what happened to him when he came home after a successful trip. He walked in the house feeling rather good. When his wife greeted him, she asked him to please take out the trash. When she noticed that he was having a difficult time "re-entering" life, she said, "You may be God's man of faith and power out there, but when you come home you're the garbage man." That has an amazing way of aiding our re-entry.

When we were in Arizona two years ago, a prophet gave Beni and me a word. It was quite extensive and 100 percent accurate. He mentioned that we were to build a new building and that even though I didn't want to, God wasn't asking for my permission. He also stated that I would travel to places where others wouldn't want to go. I find that interesting, especially as I consider a trip that I have coming up to Round Mountain, Nevada.

I'm thankful for the opportunity to travel. Yes, it's exciting for God to use me in serving the Body of Christ. That helps me grow. But because of you, there's no place like home.

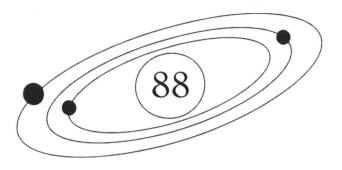

REVIVAL IN MALAWI

"We are in revival!" These are the words I heard this past week from Mike Chandler, our missionary to Malawi, Africa. If you know anything about what a true revival is, you understand that this is a very bold claim.

Following my conversation with the enthused missionary, I couldn't help but get excited too. I was in Malawi two and a half years ago. There were the beginnings of revival then. Birth pangs. I spoke at two pastors' conferences and their district council, which is a gathering of pastors and churches from about one third of the nation. God moved in a very powerful way. We saw mass healings and, more importantly, a reception to God's word for the moment. It was encouraging to be in the place where there was so much hunger for God. While the birth pangs were evident, there was a needed breakthrough in several areas. I've been told that has happened.

On July 29, Steve Thompson and I leave for Africa again. This time I've been given an even greater privilege. They have asked me to be the speaker at their general council, which is the meeting of pastors and their congregations from the entire nation. On top of that, I may be involved in another pastors' conference, depending on flight schedules, as well as a very special chance to speak in two private sessions to the presbytery of the nation. That is the group of pastors who oversee the ministry for the whole nation. Missionary leaders will be in attendance from all over the continent of Africa.

Here's the catch. I need what they have. And yet, when I prayed about God's direction, I was clearly to go. Therefore I am believing that God will enable me to serve them well, plus be able to bring home some of what they have that I—we—need. Please pray. *Please* pray.

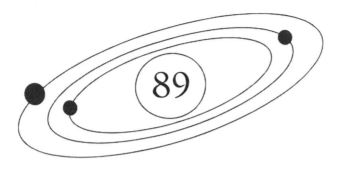

CALLING AFRICA

It's Friday morning. This day has started like most others—rising early, taking a shower (making sure that there is still life in these bones), praying in the Spirit (praying with understanding is difficult that time of day), getting ready for the prayer meeting, getting ready for the day. My thoughts eventually turn to my "to do" list, and then to my "wish I could do" list. Probably like you, I begin to think about a variety of things—the person who needs help but won't receive it, bills that are due, and how I'm going to juggle things this month. Typical thoughts. Perhaps too typical.

When I sat down at my desk, I saw a note that I was to call Africa. My mind quickly changed gears—I've been invited to teach at the General Council of the Assemblies of God in Malawi, Africa, (with Mike and Lynn Chandler). I also have the chance to teach at pastors' conferences in Tanzania, Africa, (with Ron and Gloria Hansen).

My recent conversation with Ron was very interesting. He had just returned from the "bush" where he had preached the gospel to an unreached tribe. They lived as people did a thousand years ago. They had never planted a seed, raised an animal, or even lived indoors (not even mud huts!), and had never heard the name Jesus. Many from this tribe of 5,000 were converted, with ten being baptized in the Holy Spirit.

I finally called Mike in Malawi. It was great to hear his voice and to hear how his family was doing. My visit of 1989 seemed like only yesterday, as the sights and sounds of hungry Africans are forever etched on my mind.

Now what were those typical thoughts again? They don't seem to have quite the impact of an hour ago. I wonder why?

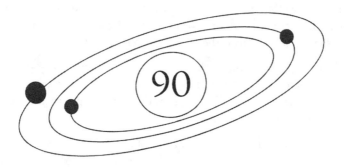

LOVE, NOT POLITICAL PRESSURE

I wrote a letter to the editor of our local paper this past week. In it I expressed concern over the fact that the leaders of some service organizations had chosen to hold our Fourth of July Parade on a Sunday morning. I believe that keeping a day of rest is an important part of life. Equal in importance is the need to maintain standards of respect by a community for the values and practices of the church. That was my reason for the letter.

Several months ago I was approached by one of those leaders about my opinion regarding the parade on Sunday. I expressed my thoughts. I appreciated their desire to get a pastor's input, something they didn't have to do. However, they chose to disregard my convictions. But there was never any harsh words or disrespect on either side, then or now.

I received a phone call this week from the same leader. He was upset because of the coalition of pastors that had formed to apply pressure upon them and possibly stir up the people to undermine this activity for the community. I'm not quoting him—that is my interpretation.

While there isn't such a movement, I understand how they could feel that way. The letters have been numerous, and many comments have been less than kind. One very difficult lesson for us to learn is to know how to disagree agreeably. It's true that several of the pastors have talked and have been upset that the church's schedule didn't seem to influence their decision, but there hasn't been and will not be a political uprising from the Christian community to undermine those who serve us. We must graciously give input and then pray. Stay away from manipulation.

The church should be involved in helping to establish public policy. We must care enough about our community's activities to give our input. We have something to offer the community through our work, our service, and our ideas. But we are not to run things. Why? It would distract us from our real mission and give us the wrong idea of power. Taking the gospel to the nations is the priority. Don't be distracted.

I've apologized to my friend in the service organization for any offense or trouble that my letter may have caused. And just as I publicly and privately disagree with the decision to have the parade on Sunday, I publicly and privately support them for the job they are doing, and I'm thankful for them.

Please do the same. Our strength is not in political pressure. Our mission is to show the love of Christ to the world, whether that be the natives in Africa or those who work so hard to serve our community. We owe them our respect.

LEAVING FOR BETHEL

Bethel voted on us last Sunday night. "Ninety-six percent...a landslide! That's unheard of in a church this size," we were told. The good news: God confirmed what we felt He was directing us to do. The hard news—our leaving Weaverville is official.

I have been mourning the possibility of this move for six months. The last four weeks have been extremely difficult. Sorrow is natural and OK. However, I have felt the conviction of the Holy Spirit about my mourning. For me it had gotten to a place where it dishonored God. I am confident that God has spoken, and He has promised good things for both my family and this church. How that is to happen is up to Him. But He can be trusted.

This last week was very encouraging. While attending a conference in Redding, I was approached by many local pastors. Each one told me that they had been praying for Bethel Church. Many felt that God has led them to pray that I would be chosen as Bethel's new pastor. God's word to us has been affirmed over and over again. I'm so thankful.

Two weeks ago, Dick Joyce came and ministered to us again. He has been the most faithful mobile ministry that this church family has known. His word to us is very important. He spoke much needed words to us about this season of change. Hear them. Embrace them.

On Dick's second day with us, he prophesied over this church. Below is a portion of that word:

> God has not changed His mind regarding any prophecy over this church—not one! Very often, while God chooses L.A., Toronto, etc., He chooses the out-of-the-way places saying, "I'm going to establish in this place a role model (the fivefold ministry will go out from this church) for a larger city to follow."

What is happening is more than a change of pastors. They (Bill and Beni) go as apostles from this church, and will continue to bear apostolic relationship to this church. God is raising up the first apostolic ministry that will rise up and go out of this place.

This is the same basic word that the leadership of this flock received from God about this transition. God has been so good to confirm this word to us through someone as trustworthy as Dick Joyce.

Remember, Israel was told to *"put your trust in His prophets and succeed"* (2 Chron. 20:20 NASB). This is a wonderful day. As we share the sorrows that this change brings, let's not forget to share the joys and remember the promises. It honors God for us to do so. Jesus said, *"My food is to do the will of Him who sent Me"* (John 4:34 NASB). Considering that analogy, I've just been given a big plate full of food. I have to remember that the will of God is like a big dinner—delicious and satisfying.

GOOD-BYE TO WEAVERVILLE

Perhaps the most difficult words to express are those that are labeled "final." In this farewell, I want to pay, at least in part, my debt of thanks to you, the family I love. (When tears flow, words don't. And so, I write instead of speak.)

Thank you for giving my family space—the room to be a normal family. Not all pastors have it so good.

Thank you for giving my children a chance to grow up without the undue pressures of being "preacher's kids." Some pastors' children are destroyed by people's unrealistic expectations. You avoided that trap, and enabled mine to thrive.

Thanks for allowing Beni to be a wife and mother first. The kids and I needed that. The pastor's wife is often a target of much criticism and judgment. Because you were never that way, she flourishes!

Thank you for giving me room to grow. When many saints discover the blemishes of their leaders, the outcome isn't a pretty sight. You are the exception.

Thanks for listening to me. You honored me by doing so, and have exalted the Word of God to its rightful place in the church. You hear and do. Because of you I have been the envy of others.

Thank you for staying with us during the dark seasons. Many find it hard to stay with a body of believers through all the seasons. You did. And so, together we laughed and wept, danced and plodded.

Thank you for giving to us. We entrusted our lives to you; and you were careful, as well as generous. When we were in crisis, you were there. When we were in need, you gave to us, often out of your own need.

Thank you for not requiring me to be perfect. It's a fairly long walk from here.

Thanks for being our friends. Not many pastors have real friends.

You have helped us raise our kids. You've put food on our table and clothes on our backs. You have given us the rare opportunity to live in a community like Weaverville. Most of all, for what we have given to you, you have given us Jesus in return. In all that you have done for us, we say, thank you...a million times, thank you!

Please continue now in these things, that you might honor God for His generous gift to you—the Silk family.

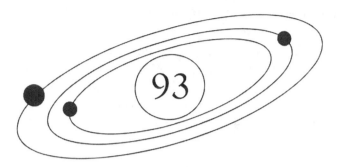

GRIEVING IN CHANGE

That was it—a very simple message from God that would define His direction for this church family. We started the year with an awareness that God was about to do something new. I'm not always the most eager for change, but I love *new*—especially *God's new.* Throughout this year we have seen change. And each time it seemed like we were making a payment into an account called *The Lordship of Jesus.* This has all been done in surrender to His will, knowing that He rewards us for obedience and personal sacrifice.

We rejoiced together in the privilege of sending out many families in ministry—some in starting two new churches, some to missions, and still others going out in support roles elsewhere in the Body of Christ. Most of the ones we sent out were part of our ministry core. I've always believed that if I'm going to err, I want to err on the side of generosity. Giving over 50 percent of our core has been costly. But we've never yet been able to out-give God. Since we started sending people out into service, He has provided more new believers in a ten-month period of time than in the previous ten years combined. God has responded to our actions with a loud, "Amen!"

This past fall we were finally able to start our building project. Unquestionably, we felt that this would be an occasion when the Lord would honor us for our willingness to embrace change. And He did. The gift of $50,000 the day before we were to actually start the fund-raising process—for that exact amount of money—was a great confirmation to the direction that we believed God had given to us. While the amount for the whole project hasn't come in yet, we know that He will complete what He started.

Renewal has come to Weaverville. This is really the ultimate change, as it deals with more than *where we live* and *what kind of building we meet in.* This is a change of heart, one that is spiritual in nature. This renewal is preparing us for the coming revival, which has been our heart's cry for years. God has answered that cry with renewal. This is the Father's blessing.

Then the unbelievable happened, a change that few of us were expecting—my move from Weaverville. It's difficult to express how hard this is for us. I've talked with many of you, and feel for you and your difficulty in sorting through the mixed emotions that have surfaced through my announcement. I don't fault anyone for feeling bad. I've had six months to process this whole thing, and I'm still struggling. I deal with it by keeping things simple. *He has never failed, and He is in charge.*

In every area that He has required change, He has blessed us. Will He now forget His promises? Is He blessing us here because I am here? Absolutely not, on both counts! We have obeyed God, and have enjoyed His favor. But even in obedience, we don't earn His blessing. He has blessed simply because He is good.

To be able to deal with the issues that are before us, we must remember a couple of ongoing essentials. First, God is the Sovereign Lord. He rules over all, and nothing escapes His notice. The greatness of His work is in no way linked to the greatness of man's abilities or resources. Second, He has never been surprised. He knows what's coming, and has prepared Himself to care for us when we've become nervous, insecure, or surprised. Third, His promises never fail. His word over this church family is not linked to one person. His will is much bigger than any one of us.

These essentials are to help us deal with the most dreaded part of change—the feeling of hopelessness. There is great hope in this because God is the Author. He always takes us from "faith to faith," from "glory to glory" and from "strength to strength." He only moves forward.

Granted, the things that I've mentioned don't help with grief. But then, grief is not wrong. It's not a sign of unbelief—or anything else that's negative. It's a sign of love. We hurt because we love. How can we deal with our grief? First, by admitting that it's there. Don't pretend it doesn't exist. Second, in your grief, invite the Holy Spirit, the Comforter, to come and soothe your heart. Give Him the opportunity to come and heal. Third, be generous in your expression of love for people. We never know how long they will be in our lives. Fourth, hunger for Heaven. Regardless of how temporal this life is, we know that we will spend eternity together. No one has ever gone wrong by seeking *"those things which are above"* (Col. 3:1). Let's help each other with this transition.

AUTHOR CONTACT INFORMATION

BILL JOHNSON

Bethel Church

933 College View Drive

Redding, CA 96003

www.BJM.org

www.iBethel.org

RECOMMENDED READING

Here Comes Heaven by Bill Johnson and Mike Seth

Basic Training for the Prophetic Ministry by Kris Vallotton

Basic Training for the Supernatural Ways of Royalty by Kris Vallotton

Developing a Supernatural Lifestyle by Kris Vallotton

Loving Our Kids On Purpose by Danny Silk

Purity—The New Moral Revolution by Kris Vallotton

The Happy Intercessor by Beni Johnson

The Supernatural Ways of Royalty by Kris Vallotton and Bill Johnson

The Ultimate Treasure Hunt by Kevin Dedmon

Spiritual Java by Bill Johnson, Beni Johnson, Kris Vallotton,
Kevin Dedmon, Danny Silk, Banning Liebscher

In the right hands, This Book will Change Lives!

Most of the people who need this message will not be looking for this book. To change their lives, you need to put a copy of this book in their hands.

> *But others (seeds) fell into good ground, and brought forth fruit, some a hundred-fold, some sixty-fold, some thirty-fold* (Matthew 13:8).

Our ministry is constantly seeking methods to find the good ground, the people who need this anointed message to change their lives. Will you help us reach these people?

> *Remember this—a farmer who plants only a few seeds will get a small crop. But the one who plants generously will get a generous crop* (2 Corinthians 9:6).

EXTEND THIS MINISTRY BY SOWING
3 BOOKS, 5 BOOKS, 10 BOOKS, **OR MORE TODAY,**
AND BECOME A LIFE CHANGER!

Thank you,

Don Nori Sr., Publisher
Destiny Image
Since 1982